Journal of Beat Studies

Volume 8, 2020

PACE UNIVERSITY PRESS • NEW YORK

Copyright © 2020 by
Pace University Press
41 Park Row, 15th Floor
New York, NY 10038

All rights reserved
Printed in the United States of America

ISSN 2165-8706
ISBN: 978-1-935625-48-3 (pbk: alk.ppr.)

Member

Council of Editors of Learned Journals

♾ Paper used in this publication meets the minimum requirements of American National Standard for Information Sciences–Permanence of Paper for Printed Library Materials, ANSI Z39.48–1984

Editors

Ronna C. Johnson — Tufts University
Nancy M. Grace — The College of Wooster (emerita)

Book Review Editor

Matt Theado — Kobe City University of Foreign Sudies (Kobe, Japan)

Editorial Board

Ann Charters — University of Connecticut–Storrs (emerita)
Maria Damon — Pratt Institute of Art
Terence Diggory — Skidmore College (emeritus)
Tim Gray — CUNY Staten Island
Oliver Harris — Keele University, United Kingdom
Allen Hibbard — Middle Tennessee State University
Tim Hunt — Illinois State University
A. Robert Lee — The University of Murcia, Spain
Cary Nelson — University of Illinois
Jennie Skerl — West Chester University (retired)
David Sterritt — Long Island University (emeritus)
Tony Trigilio — Columbia College Chicago
John Whalen-Bridge — National University of Singapore, Singapore

Production Staff

Delaney Anderson — Graduate Assistant, Pace University Press
Francesca Leparik — Graduate Assistant, Pace University Press

Journal of Beat Studies

Volume 8, 2020

	1	Letter from the Editors
Timothy Gray	5	"Take it Easier": Joanne Kyger in Bolinas
Jane Falk	21	Joanne Kyger's Poetics: Finding the Continuous Thread
Aldon Lynn Nielsen	41	Ted Talk
Katherine Kinney	49	Improvisation c. 1959: Beat Film

SURVEY

	67	State-of-the-Field Survey of Beat Studies Scholars

REVIEWS

John Shapcott	95	*The Green Ghost: William Burroughs and the Ecological Mind* by Chad Weidner
Tony Trigilio	100	*Straight Around Allen: On the Business of Being Allen Ginsberg* by Bob Rosenthal
Allan Johnston	105	*Approaches to Teaching Baraka's* Dutchman edited by Matthew Calihman and Gerald Early
Mary Paniccia Carden	110	*Diane di Prima: Visionary Poetics and the Hidden Religions* by David Stephen Calonne

117	The Beat Index
131	In Memoriam: Michael McClure
133	Essay Abstracts
135	Notes on Contributors
137	Editorial Policy

Letter from the Editors

This volume is a departure from previous ones. We elected to forego our usual Beat Interview and to feature instead a survey of Beat Studies scholars on the topic of the state of the field. The field has changed dramatically since its mid-twentieth-century genesis, and as we saw ourselves approaching the tenth volume of the journal (forthcoming 2022) we thought it apropos to see what our colleagues are thinking about the field—its viability now and in the future. The responses you find in this volume reflect a cross-section of working scholars associated with the Beat Studies Association, some relatively new to the field and others with long and storied careers as experts in Beat literature and the arts. Their statements acknowledge that the field is still not fully recognized, although genuine strides have been made to contextualize Beat literature in U.S. and world literature, revealing the historical and cultural forces promoting and sustaining avant-garde literatures. These scholars speak to the importance of rigorous research methods; to the need for more research exploring race, gender, and class dynamics; to the importance of pedagogical discussions; and to the need for more attention to transnational elements of Beat discourses.

All academic fields need this kind of discussion, an assessment among peers of the value of their work and the processes necessary to sustain the academic project. At the very least, this survey of the field creates a community of scholars whose work depends upon the linkages in Beat scholarship that bind them.

This feature in the *Journal* also serves as special acknowledgement of Jennie Skerl, one of the field's most influential scholars, particularly her ground-breaking work on William S. Burroughs and her editing of *Reconstructing the Beats* (2004) and the *Transnational Beat Generation* (Palgrave 2012). She is also the founder of the Beat Studies Association (BSA), and without her seminal idea for an association and her leadership as its first president, the *Journal of Beat Studies*, a major project supported by the BSA, would not exist. She retired in 2008 as associate dean for the College of Arts and Sciences at West Chester University (West Chester, PA) but has continued as an active scholar, writing reviews for the *Journal* and editing the collected interviews of Ed Sanders, forthcoming this fall from Clemson UP/Liverpool UP as the inaugural volume in its new Beat Studies Book Series.

The remainder of the volume features two essays on the poetry of the late Joanne Kyger. In "'Take It Easier': Joanne Kyger in Bolinas," Tim Gray, who has published on Gary Snyder and Diane di Prima and is currently working on a monograph on Kyger, reflects on Kyger's Bolinas-inspired poetry and end-of-life concerns in a time of ecological crisis. Jane Falk, who has written on Philip Whalen, Michael McClure, as well as Kyger, complements Gray's essay in "Joanne Kyger's Poetics: Finding the Continuous Thread" by elucidating Kyger's composition practices. This includes her use of open form poetics, appropriation, epigrams, serial poems, the practice of Buddhism, and the influence of poets such as Charles Olson and Jack Spicer. Falk concludes that Kyger most consistently dealt with the practice of writing rather than its final product.

These two essays are complemented by Aldon Lynn Nielsen's "Ted Talk" on poet Ted Joans and the concept of the hipster, a survey of sorts that reveals Joans's political, economic, and aethestic projects as an amalgamation of grass-root capitalism (e.g., Rent-a-Beatnik), his political take-down of Mailer's white hipster via collage art (*The Hipsters*), and his transnational travels, a life's journey that Nielsen claims took Joans from hipster, to hippie, to what he calls the more recent "farcical" version of the first. The section concludes with Katherine Kinney's "Improvisation c. 1959: Beat Film," an essay that conjoins discussion of Jonas Mekas's ground-breaking writing on experimental film with Kinney's analysis of Robert Frank and Alfred Leslie's *Pull My Daisy*, John Cassavetes's *Shadows*, Mekas's *Guns of the Trees,* and Shirley Clarke's *The Connection*. The essay stresses the various (and sometimes misleading) ways the term *improvisational* has been used, while elucidating the innovative efforts of these directors to defy Hollywood convention, especially through the casting of non-actors and African Americans.

As always, the volume features reviews of recent research on Beat and Beat-associated authors, this time including Allan Johnston on *Approaches to Teaching Baraka's* Dutchman, edited by Matthew Calihman and Gerald Early; John Shapcott on Chad Weidner's *The Green Ghost: William Burroughs and the Ecological Mind*; Mary Paniccia Carden on Stephen David Calonne's *Diane di Prima: Visionary Poetics and the Hidden Religions*; and Tony Trigilio on Bob Rosenthal's *Straight Around Allen: On the Business of Being Allen Ginsberg*.

The volume concludes with the Beat Index, which we hope continues to support scholars in the field by disseminating a clear and viable path of prior research upon which we can further develop Beat Studies.

****

We would be remiss if we did not mark here the historical moment of our time. As a result of the COVID-19 pandemic, many of you have faced the disruption of your classrooms and the need to retool face-to-face teaching to online instruction; social isolation orders and obligatory quarantine; the postponement of primary elections; economic turmoil; and the fact that the nation was grossly misled regarding the severity of the virus. This new reality has been exacerbated by what many have called an "inflection point" in U.S. race relations: mass demonstrations in opposition to systemic racism, galvanized by the murder of George Floyd by a Minneapolis police officer in May. The recent unjustified

LETTERS FROM THE EDITORS

killings of Rayshard Brooks, Ahmaud Arbery, and Breonna Taylor, among others, have forced many to recognize the systemic function of white militarized policing of people of color—and calls for systemic reform. We must keep working to erase those inequities, and as you read this, our best hope is that we can be a genuine catalyst for change, no matter how long that arc toward justice truly is.

    Onward!

Ronna C. Johnson   Nancy M. Grace

"Take It Easier": Joanne Kyger in Bolinas
Timothy Gray

Described by Robert Creeley as "whimsically tough" ("Introduction" 104), Joanne Kyger occupied a pivotal position in the development of open poetics in the latter half of the twentieth century. Excluded from Donald Allen's 1960 anthology, *The New American Poetry*, Kyger nonetheless represented the nascent movement's experimental tenets and could easily have been included in four of the "five large groups" Allen delineated in the anthology's preface. By the late 1950s, Kyger had already established ties with the Black Mountain poets, the San Francisco Renaissance poets, the Beat Generation poets, and a separate group with "no geographical definition," which included, along with her future husband Gary Snyder and her close friend Philip Whalen, "younger poets who have been associated with and in some cases influenced by the leading writers of the preceding groups" (Allen xiii). Kyger had not yet made contact with the New York Poets, the fifth group Allen mentioned, but she would in time become close allies with their so-called "second-generation," appearing in their small press publishing ventures and welcoming them to northern California when they joined the hippie generation's back-to-the-land exodus. It was there, in Bolinas, California, located on an isolated coastal inlet north of San Francisco, that Kyger honed her literary voice and elevated her status as an open-minded intellectual attuned to rhythms of everyday life.

Kyger moved to Bolinas in the spring of 1969. She was 35 years old. Midlife was for her a period of revival and enlightenment, a chance to experience freedoms denied her, and other counterculture women, in earlier decades. In Bolinas, Kyger's poetry grew more reflective and personal, even as she retained the foundational influences of groups delineated in Allen's anthology. She emerged as one of the few writers who could inject into an otherwise calm discussion of Buddhist equanimity her personal quirks and anxieties, which is another way of saying that Joanne Kyger kept things real. Her talent is formidable, and her poetry can be complex, but she remains one of our most approachable avant-garde writers. Indeed, to read Kyger is to feel the attraction one has towards a friend. She is honest, fun, and creative to the core.

In this essay, I offer a brief examination of how Kyger (and her writing) flourished in Bolinas, long after the Beat and hippie eras had passed. For Kyger, open poetics had already accommodated a range of experiences and emotions, but in Bolinas a place-based approach provided newfound solace and grounding, key attributes as she settled into her later career. As announced in one poem, she learned how to "take it easier" without compromising her avant-garde edge. Despite her laid-back demeanor, Kyger was a highly attentive poet, tracking interconnected beings in natural and spiritual realms, seeking rhythmic balance in a coastal climate, and (in accord with her Buddhist practice) discerning form in formlessness.

Kyger's move from Santa Barbara to San Francisco in 1957, a dozen years prior to her encampment in Bolinas, set her on a path of poetic experimentation. She arrived in San Francisco during heady times. The San Francisco Renaissance was already "kind of 'over,'" Kyger recalled in conversation with Linda Russo, but she found the Bay Area reinvigorated by an "other phenomenon," namely the literary refugees from Black Mountain College, an experimental inter-arts mecca in North Carolina that had recently closed its doors (Russo, "Interview"). Literary critics have long noted Kyger's involvement with Jack Spicer and Robert Duncan, who invited her to their Sunday literary circle, accepted her on their literary "boys' team," and promoted her work to Don Allen (Russo, "How You Want" 22, 28). Beat biographers usually mention Kyger's brief marriage to Gary Snyder, and her long friendship with Philip Whalen. Curiously, though, not as much has been said about Kyger's contact with Robert Creeley, John Wieners, Paul Alexander, Joe Dunn, Tom Field, Bill McNeil, and other Black Mountain castoffs who migrated to San Francisco in the late 1950s.[1] It's also crucial to mention her contacts with Bill Berkson, Joe Brainard, and other members of the New York School in the early 1970s. Indeed, although Kyger is regularly classified as a Beat writer, her affiliations and influences were not limited to Beat circles, nor should they have been, as she often admonished interviewers.[2] In this regard, Mary Paniccia Carden's description of Diane di Prima seems just as apt when we talk about Kyger: "Rather than joining already-established Beat communities, she gravitates toward those who open themselves to life without premeditated plans or parameters; for her, it is a matter of course that she creates community with artists and writers who value pure, unregulated experience as 'the ultimate good'" (Carden 51).

In addition to the countercultural aspects of the New American Poetry, it was avant-garde poetics that appealed to Kyger, and in the Black Mountain poets she found useful guides. As Creeley said of his cohort, "We were trying to think of how a more active sense of poetry might be got....We were trying in effect to think of a base, or a different base from which to move." Addressing the same aesthetic focus, Joel Oppenheimer said, "I think we're more interested in the line, in the formal use of the line than say, the Beats or the New York poets" (Duberman, 414). John Wieners urged Kyger to disregard mistakes and to resist re-writing for the sake of the line's breath (Smith, "Energy"). Especially influential to Kyger's early poetic development was "Projective Verse," the statement on poetics written in 1950 by Black Mountain College's rector, Charles Olson (and reprinted a decade later in *The New American Poetry*). Based on Kyger's varied recollections, "Projective Verse" was put into her hands either by Wieners (Carolan 26) or by fellow Black Mountaineer Joe Dunn (Russo, "Interview"). Regardless of who handed it to her, Kyger saw in Olson's manifesto "a way of looking at writing and the page" (Carolan, 26). She read "Projective Verse" repeatedly. "There was a field, an energy, energy on the page," she said of Olson's work. "The page itself was an energy source, and words and ideas were transmitted to it. As quick as ideas arrived they should be transformed into this field" (Smith and Price, 106). Kyger continued to read this landmark essay while living in Japan. "Olson's PROJECTIVE VERSE hits me like a whallop," she wrote in a 1960 journal entry (*Japan* 60).

Olson's bold emphasis on breath units shaped Kyger's early work, especially her feminist epic, *The Tapestry and the Web*. Yet Michael Davidson adds a relevant proviso: "If Kyger drew the shape of her line from long poems like Olson's *Maximus Poems* or Gary Snyder's *Mountains and Rivers Without End*, she also understood that their historical and cultural concerns could not be hers" (192). Fortunately, the younger Black Mountain exiles suggested to Kyger a quieter, subtler, but no less adventurous, blend of life and artistry. Recalling her first meeting with Paul Alexander in San Francisco in 1958, after an introduction by Tom Field, Kyger says, "His small abode looks like a tiny palace—like his later places. Books, pottery, plants, tiny treasures, paintings, drawings, sculpture. There is always excellent talk at the slow dinners. The table becomes the world." The friendly confines and relaxed pace of Alexander's bohemian domicile shaped the experimental art that is made there. "When Paul draws," Kyger notes, "it is with an intimate line, quick, moving, a body, a horizon. There are many beautiful drawings and watercolors, paintings of gleaming, creamy colors" ("Buzz Time," *There You Are* 33). Whereas Olson mentioned oceanic SPACE as his (epic) starting point, Kyger suggests that Alexander's "tiny palace" in North Beach provides an alternative vantage point, another way of approaching the horizon. So, too, does the "intimate line" of Alexander's art. Throughout the 1960s, Kyger searched for a similar zone, a place of "slow dinners" and artistic exchange, and a corresponding intimacy in her poetic line. Over the course of a decade, she lived in Japan, traveled to Europe, and attempted to live in New York City, but she could not find her true rhythm. Only when she settled in Bolinas, on a mesa overlooking the Pacific, did she realize, in full, her humble spiritual quest.

Joanne Kyger in Bolinas, c. 2000. Photo Credit: Thomas L. Milligan

Kyger's poetry became more supple and playful—less epic, if you will—once she dissolved her ego in coastal California's natural beauty.[3] As Linda Russo says, "Reading Kyger, we become familiar with the porousness of life atop the mesa" ("Precious" 28). The young woman who longed for a room of her own while living with Snyder in Japan found an even more expansive environment on the California coast (Kyger, *Japan* 31). Creeley, who moved to Bolinas in the early 1970s, marveled at the harmonious balance Kyger achieved. "She lives so explicitly where she is and with what she has as a daily factor," Creeley noted, "that some projection of it all into the vacant generality of usual ambitions has never been her interest" ("A note" vii). As Kyger herself said of *Joanne* (1970), her first volume of verse composed entirely in Bolinas: "the 'individual' is swept out to sea, a group location identity, a place, takes precedence as voice" (Waldman and Warsh 590). Kyger underscored this message in *Places to Go* (also published in 1970), understanding her writing self in egoless relation to natural elements: "the grass springs back, a vehicle/ for what passes through/ Not for identity of I's and sorrows/ Struck by humility total of truth/ Listening to separate existence of worlds" (*About Now* 193). Truth, for Kyger, involved paring down meaning to its easiest applications. In a quotidian poem like "Tuesday, October 28, 1969, Bolinas," that meant writing letters, sweeping the floor, and making plans to wash hair. In "October 28, Take It Easier," that meant abandoning that day's household tasks for the beach: "The sand/ will be warm, I'm sure/ for the sun is out today, and although not warm/ in the house/ It is in the spot I am going to now" (186). This kind of free verse really was free. Charlie Vermont recalled that Kyger was "not in awe of the great ego-maniacs abounding during those 'expansive times,'" and that in Bolinas she rebounded from her previous subservience to Snyder and Ginsberg to cultivate her own "disciplined openness" (Vermont, "Letter"), evident in her resolve to "take it easier." Gone were the days of uncertainty Kyger recorded in *The Japan and India Journals*, when she said, "I am neither open nor closed/ a/ leaky faucet (*Japan* 13). Sprung loose in Bolinas, Kyger could tap natural fluidity as she wished, and refashion her poetry accordingly.

For the sake of contrast, let's look at an early poem, written in Japan and incorporated into *The Tapestry and the Web*, which shows the hesitancy that once plagued Kyger. Gathering well water for a bath, drinking gin, and feeling blue, she muses:

> ... Have I lost all values I wonder
> the world is slippery to hold on to
>
> When you begin to deny it.
>
> Outside outside are the crickets and frogs in the rice fields
>
> Large black butterflies like birds. (*About Now* 71)

Struggling to acculturate herself to Japan while Snyder is pursuing his Buddhist studies, Kyger appears lost, but she implies that she's ready to be found. She knows that denying the world makes that world hard to grasp, and she emphasizes her personal disconnect with a conspicuous enjambment across a stanza break. The ensuing single-line stanzas imply that she stands at a remove from the natural world, a separation doubly felt when she repeats the word "outside." Kyger is not so disoriented by the haze of loneliness to ignore the mysterious sounds and sights of other living creatures (crickets, frogs, and butterflies), but neither does she fully commune with these sentient beings, which are full of the Buddha nature; in fact, she regards the natural world as "slippery."[4] She is, however, edging closer to her environment and using her writing journal to sort through her shifting perceptions and literary aspirations. When she was "living and breathing in Japan," she later recalled in a roundtable discussion at Naropa, "paying attention to the details of daily life became a part of what [she] perceived as Zen…they didn't become the mundane thing of the 'housewife'" ("Women and the Beats" 54).[5] Attentiveness is Kyger's hallmark, but it can take on a different character, depending on her situation.

Broadly speaking, Kyger's early poetry incorporates her attentiveness rather differently than does her later work. In *The Tapestry and the Web*, for instance, Kyger asserts that there is "nothing promised that isn't shown" (*About Now* 62), betraying a wary, self-protective tone, though also a spur to action. Throughout *Tapestry*, she developed a prosodic style, a warp and weft, that helped her weave a new feminist myth. "I put a straight line down the middle and made everything branch off it like a tree," Kyger told an arts panel in 1974. She went on to explain that the poetic line in *Tapestry* "had its roots on the ground and then things branch off from either side of it. You could fit all the voices and patterns that got into the movement that way" ("Kent State Arts Panel," *There You Are* 88). *Tapestry* is a polyvocal weave of disparate energies, the linear organization of which helps recalibrate traditional notions of heroism. Compared to Kyger's later work, the lines in *Tapestry* may seem busy, and their articulation a bit abstract, but the revisionist myth in this volume finds balance thanks to Kyger's organic conception of craft.

By the time she settled in Bolinas, Kyger was pursuing deliberate focus rather than busy movement. "At this point the kind of space that interests me is the kind of space that vibrates its meaning," she told the arts panel. "It's the one-liner or the sampler on the wall. It just stays there for a long time. You can go back into that one line and it will keep giving off overtones" (89). Living in a yurt with her second husband, Jack Boyce (Schneider 109), staying in the Grand Hotel with Bill Berkson (Waldman and Warsh 575), and eventually settling into a house Boyce built, Kyger became more of an active seer, open to the promises abounding in nature. Granted, the highs she recorded occasionally involved recreational drugs, abundant in those days, but she adopted a responsible perspective. "At the time many of us were seekers," Charlie Vermont remembers. "Joanne had been doing it a long time. She was sane when many in the vicinity were not….Joanne was an adult who was living a different life than the average person, so she made other choices more believable." (Vermont, "Letter"). Kyger has talked openly about her rituals, suggesting that taking drugs helped her move on from "habit patterns" and "linear space" to consider "phrases… that have some internal turning, that seem to turn around all the time. So it even gets out of meaning after a while, it gets into being a mantra or it just hangs in a different way in the air." Transported by hallucinogenic drugs to situations "outside of usual time," she grasped in Bolinas a "mythic" story quite different from the myth she crafted in *Tapestry*, hearing the birds twitter while noticing that "another kind of chatter had ceased" (Nahem 67-68, 73). The poems in *Joanne*, especially, drift toward languor, but we are aware that Kyger's mind is constantly flashing.

Telling in this regard is a pair of poems Kyger addressed to Joe Brainard, an artist and writer associated with the New York School. Brainard visited Bolinas in the summer of 1971, reuniting with New York school friends like Ted Berrigan, who had decamped there, and instantly gushing over Kyger, whom he was meeting for this first time: "Everyone said I was going to love Joanne Kyger and I do, I do!" (Brainard, *Bolinas Journal* n.p.). Their friendship lasted for years. In an undated poem, Kyger describes an afternoon in 1980 in New York City, during which she and Brainard consumed so many Bloody Mary's and Quaaludes that she was unable to assemble a collage ("Joe Brainard," *There You Are* 118). In another poem, composed in January 1994, when Brainard, suffering from AIDS, was barely clinging to life, Kyger shifts the scene of their friendship back to California in 1971, recalling "the acid trip in Bo/ when we sat under the french broom/ and looked at the tiny peapod seeds,/ the shining eucalyptus leaves/ oily and flashing in the sun" ("January 7–June 25th 1994 (for Joe)," *There You Are* 119). Bo was the local nickname of Bolinas, although the image of Buddha experiencing enlightenment under the Bodhi ("Bo") tree is evident both in the moniker of the town and in the position of the zonked-out friends sitting underneath a french broom shrub.[6] As the drugs start to take hold, Kyger and Brainard are treated to "The natural/ haphazard casual toss/ of offerings from the beach/ shore line harmoniously positioned/ together in framed collages" ("January 7," *There You Are* 119). Although in real time it was offered a decade prior, this gift from the sea (or, perhaps, the fond memory of it) effectively completes the collage Kyger could not finish on her own in New York City in 1980. Kyger's recollection resonates all the more when we consider that Brainard, the New York School's most acclaimed collagist, was by her side at both events.[7] Of course, the coastline of Bolinas also figures prominently in her artistic success.

Joanne Kyger in Bolinas, c. 2000.
Photo Credit: Thomas L. Milligan

Indeed, it was natural rhythm, more than any drug-induced trance, that affected Kyger's consciousness and shaped her poetry. "Often I try so hard with stimulants/ which only graze the surface... // Whereas the real state is called golden/ where things are exactly what they are," she remarked in an early 1970s poem (*About*

Now 285). In Bolinas, joy was immediate and palpable. Kyger marveled, early and often, that she "was no longer in waiting as this world I called/ my own opened out" (249). Immersed in the beauty of the Golden State, witnessing tidal dispersals along its coast, she seized upon environmental detail with the zeal of a painter or a photographer, even though she wasn't one, and with the empathy of a practicing Buddhist, which she was.

In 1989, Kyger addressed that dynamic directly by answering her own question: "And so what's 'Buddhist'/ about all this // landscape consciousness/ and its fragile human frequency?/ 'The mind is as blank/ as a bone on the beach/ when the tide runs out'// Company that's what/ it's all about entwined / in the same air and walking/ in the same sun's dawn" (*About Now* 495). Through the company of friends like Brainard, and the company of natural life forms along the shore, a holistic consciousness emerged. Newly empowered, Kyger emphasized spatiality, suggesting that her coastal location was perfect for an experimental poet intent on "pushing out the horizon" (Nahem 71). Oceanic space had beckoned all along. Back in 1970, hanging out on RCA Beach with artist Arthur Okamura, Kyger had an epiphany: "Watching everything, everything happens. Inside the pace,/ well, it's rhythm & pulse, too, you meet others inside/ this flow" (219). In another early 1970s poem, the ocean assuages her personal doubts. "There is something in me which is not open,/ it does not wish to live/ it is dying," she writes. "But then in the sun, looking out to sea,/ center upon center unfold, lotus petals,/ the boundless waves of bliss" (290). The broad expanse of Pacific Rim seascape provides an appropriately fluid model for Kyger's open poetics. A clenched, anxious self can unfold in oceanic boundlessness. As happens in "Joanne," an autobiographical poem Kyger wrote during her first year in Bolinas, the seascape promises the poet and her readers a "recollected" beginning: an "ease of mind" (*About Now* 195).

Harking back to the collage work she did with Brainard, and hewing to the Buddhism she continued to study, Kyger honored the "simultaneity of all human beings on this planet,/ alive when you are alive" (378), becoming especially attuned to tiny mysteries in nature. In Bolinas, such mysteries included "crystal drops crowding the tips/ of the meadows purple grasses/ No Difference Here/ from the freshest and best" (415). While the concept of "No Difference" aligns with Buddhist notions of interconnectedness, it also reflects the palpable truths of Kyger's coastal climate. In a revelatory moment, the poet notices that she has traveled far enough off the beaten path to breathe easy: "If you make it this far you are fairly out of danger/ because now you are on foot/ on dirt roads, edged with sunlight/ and small birds. When the wind/ comes up you inhale it whole/ and slowly distribute it/ calm the torrent of breathing" (*About Now* 563). For Kyger, the confluence in this passage is subtle but revelatory, since the poetic breath unit of Olson's "Projective Verse," the meditative breathing exercise of the practicing Buddhist, and the refreshing wind that whips in from the ocean, are all of one piece. The balance of inhalation and exhalation, depicted evenly in three-beat lines, suggests an easy, stress-free continuum, rather than an epic call to action. "Ideas are a dime a dozen," Kyger told an interviewer in 1983. "I don't want that. I want to see how you live *in* your environment or in your compassion for place" (Thorpe 99). Total immersion is key to what Kyger once termed "the broad/ sweeping/ form of being there" (*About Now* 211), a state of wellness that doesn't rely on the self so much as it relies on natural phenomena surrounding the self (which subsequently dissolves in those surroundings).

As decades passed, Kyger enhanced her relationship with natural landscapes, living in Bolinas and learning in stages. In a 1997 poem, she explains that she has traded the "taut story" of "classic epics" for a looser, low-key recording of "Pacific characters," including "mammals or birds, frogs." By this juncture, it is not book knowledge that aids Kyger. Rather, it is

>   An attitude of listening repose   drifting
>   through a cumbia tea-dance with Rhamus Californica
>
>   a bushy partner
>   and an up-beat early evening towhee
>
>   who's not so wild anymore (*About Now* 643)

Rejecting epic hierarchies, Kyger regards the natural world passively, but also up close, learning in the process that living beings need not remain "wild" to one another.

The towhee is just one of many birds whose creaturely example Kyger has tracked over the years. Her 1963 poem "Look the bird is making plans" (*About Now* 83), included in a letter she sent to Philip Whalen, and later published in *Tapestry*, suggests that the time is right to leave Japan (and Snyder).[8] In the late 1980s and early 1990s, Kyger filled her "Bird Notebooks" and assorted poems with mention of migratory birds, especially the white- and gold-crown sparrows she spotted on her property. Once, when describing her residence in Bolinas, Kyger admitted, "the quail are probably my closest neighbors" (Carolan 26). In "Everyone is Flying Very Well," a poem from September 1997, Kyger appears to take courage from gold-crown sparrows, and other birds, as age encroaches:

>   Time for Robins to eat the ripe berries of the cotoneaster
>   and get gah-gah
>   Rufus sided towhees come back
>   to the same spot under the coffee-berry trees
>   to scratch and eat every year
>   See the seasonal return is confident
>
>   of itself. Confides itself in repetition
>   never quite the same. (*About Now* 642)

A creature's seasonal migration, a repetition "never quite the same," is based on self-assurance and guaranteed by place. That seems to speak to Kyger's sensibility, as well. Having a routine does not always mean getting stuck in a rut, so long as your being is enlivened on each return.

A somewhat more complicated meshing of wild nature and human consciousness arises in a poem Kyger wrote in 1996:

> The gale was upon us in a second.   Was it the dope
> brownies that made us feel so wet all
> of a sudden the space between rain
> drops was filled with rain.
> This is a serious business
> this existence thing
> this life (*About Now* 626)

As in previously cited poems, the distinction between drug vision and natural vision in Kyger's work is often hard to determine. The precariousness of the enjambed phrase "all/ of a sudden" highlights the indeterminacy of the moment. Is it the dope that suddenly takes hold and makes Kyger and her companion feel wet? Or do they get wet because the space between the raindrops is also filled with rain? Or is it the dope that makes them conscious of that filled space? No answer is immediately forthcoming, as the stanza trails off toward an existential dilemma, registered in stoner phrasing. It seems possible, though, that "this existence thing," felt keenly in the rain, derives from an ancient Buddhist precept. In the Lotus Sutra, Shakyamuni Buddha is likened to a "great cloud," and his teachings, the Dharma, to a beneficent rain pouring down steadily and indiscriminately on all creatures: "I rain down the Dharma rain,/ filling the whole world," the great sage asserts, "and this single-flavored Dharma/ is practiced by each according to the individual's power" ("Dharma Rain" 45, 48). Rather similarly, Kyger's poem witnesses "elements thundering/ down in an obligatory/ engulfing swoosh" (*About Now* 626). All are equally wet, all are equally saved, once the ego is dissolved in the natural elements (assisted by pot brownies). "What do you expect from an 'I' this morning?" Kyger asks herself in another rainy-day poem, composed a month earlier (621). Not much, she would soon learn, unless that "I" cleansed itself of ego in a downpour of Buddhist equanimity.[9]

In a 2000 poem that, in the estimation of Philip Whalen biographer David Schneider, "stands at ease with the best of Mahayana literature" (*Crowded* 125), Kyger laid bare her bodhisattva character in an affirming mantra of openness: "Your heart is fine feeling the widest/ possible empathy for the day and its inhabitants" (*About Now* 690). Even so, Kyger's empathy was challenged once human population increased in Bolinas, disturbing ecological balance. Despite all the bliss in Kyger's work, it is instructive to look at situations when natural communion and good heartedness fail to save the day. In a series of NIMBY (not-in-my-backyard) poems dating from the mid-1980s, Kyger laments that Bolinas has become spoiled by hangers-on, drug casualties, and tourists; the stylish hippies of yesteryear have been replaced by "sleazos" and "burnouts" (417). "In Memoriam" briefly invokes a local Miwok creation story, first seen in "Up My Coast" (341), only to excoriate Memorial Day tourists coming to Bolinas to see the lowest low tide in twenty years: "Place to go to, Kids… Where human feet can squish/ the living daylights out of cowering anemone/ And the local boys can *walk* to the furthest reef pool/ *pick up* their abalone and go home./ So far out, this is a view to be seen/ inside the flight of 70 black brants that didn't/ want to move, they *didn't* want to move" (539). Kyger's tone in these poems is surprisingly judgmental, but she's simply defending the environment accommodating her life and work. For coastal creatures, sustainability and balance mean everything, and Kyger is giving them a voice.

In "February 27 Sunday," an emblem poem from 1994, sea creatures continue to suffer, and Kyger is again on hand to pay witness. Off the nearby channel beach, Kyger notes that a distressed baby elephant seal, abandoned by its mother, is now forcibly fed at a rescue center. The overbearing human population of coastal California is partly to blame. About the mother seal, Kyger says,

> She was out
> of her element being young with her first birth
> which happened on the most public part
> of the town's beach.
> Around the clock watching went on until a week ago
> when she took him further north up the beach a bit
> for privacy which was not to be had.
> Horses practicing jumps, dogs, dirt bikes, curious
> humans. She leaves him in the full moon lighted waters
> This is too hard. (*About Now* 586)

By this juncture, the isolated coastal town, numbering just 500 residents when Kyger arrived in 1969, has swollen to 1500 people. The effects are felt not just by anemones and seals, but also by longstanding homesteaders. Witness Kyger's 1997 poem "I find it difficult to utter a meaningful utterance but," a screed against neighbors who park their vehicle on her property, claiming "traditional use," when it is really their non-native bottle brush overtaking their own parking space. Robert Frost could easily claim that "good fences make good neighbors," but how is a freewheeling hippie Buddhist supposed to react to these brazen boundary crossers? "I also believe gardens should be planted with native seeds," a vexed Kyger writes. "But to recommend an overview of how to sustain a floating/ immigrant population like our own, I am at a loss" (636).

More often than not, though, Kyger celebrated Bolinas as a locus of balance. Consider her miniature masterpiece, "The Fog is halfway over the mesa."

Composed in August 2001, this poem functions a bit like Wallace Stevens's "The Auroras of Autumn" or James Merrill's "The Changing Light at Sandover," tapping the fleetingness of natural phenomena to articulate an older poet's wise and wistful worldview. "My table of life for the past/ thirty years or so is not broken/ up into incidents as much as continuum," Kyger announces at the outset. A complicated linkage of inner and outer weather, so prevalent in Stevens's work, emerges here, as befits the poem's eco-centric title. The coastal fog encroaches, just as age does. It is a natural process, keeping ancient spirits around, and is made possible by:

>   the rapid combine of elements
> heretofore disparate: like Bodhidharma cruising
>   the Pacific as a   surf boarding Coyote
>   and the poor bonged-on-head disciple Naropa
>   here to meet him
>   along with the classic
>   Greco-Roman education
>   that always hauls Odysseus along. (*About Now* 719)

Lost in the fog, Bodhidharma, Coyote, Naropa, and Odysseus share the same stature, as they meet and influence each other. Kyger, too, is among their visionary company. As so often happens in California Buddhism, East meets West. It is left to discerning minds to pull spiritual magic out of the fog, for as Kyger notes, in a beautifully registered conclusion, there is

>   none of it 'indigenous' to here except
>   through conviction of the poet combining
>
>   these strands into a useful cord,   a thread
>
>   to throw into the dream and see it
>   come up clear
>   as a picture in the evening. (*About Now* 719)

Absent here is the evening star appearing in Shelley's "Adonais" or Whitman's "Lilacs," but then, this is not elegiac verse of the Western canon. We have, instead, a poet taking stock of her place in space, and of her abundant, if somewhat "disparate," influences. Kyger's clear focus of "a picture in the evening" derives from her learnedness and conviction, to be sure, but also from her abandonment of these qualities to her hazier dreams, resulting in her free and easy way of being. What Andrew Schelling says about Kyger's later poetry in general applies especially well, I think, to this poem in particular:

> The writer's mindstream is freed on the instant, and can assume a relaxed and ironic removal from the inward junk of fluctuating mood utterances; attention relocates on an out-there world: history, geopolitical observations, bioregional specifics like flora & fauna & weather currents, other people's customs, foreign vocabularies, and the indelible impact of capital on the twenty-first century. ("Joanne Kyger's Portable Poetics")

Or as Kyger herself said, the year before she composed "The Fog is halfway over the mesa":

> I feel writing is an occurrence, a happening, an intersection of the writer and time and place. The writing happens in the natural world of seasons, weather, tides. Where is the sun, where is the moon. This "real" world is there in concert with the writer's words, moods, muse. (McCreary 141)

Evident in both comments is Kyger's proclivity for combination and relocation, intersection and fluctuation. Hers is a perpetually mobile way of thinking and writing, an agile spontaneity that nonetheless resolves itself into a still point, a meditative calm.

Anchored in Bolinas, frustrated by certain demographic trends, but constantly amazed by its migratory birds, its fogs, and other natural phenomena, Kyger could rightly view her life, and the life around her, as a continuum. As the title of her first selected poems indicates, her modest-but-undeniable literary legacy is due in large part to her rhythmic adaptation, to her patience and perseverance, to simply *Going On*. For Kyger, as for Philip Whalen, writing poetry meant abandoning ambition, taking it easier, meshing with one's surroundings; it was never about individual glorification.[10] "Poetry is what we do," Whalen told Kyger in a July 1962 letter (Russo, "How You Want" 34), bucking up her spirits along with his, while implicitly rejecting the grandiose label of "poet," literary identity taking a backseat to daily practice. Forty years later, having found her rhythm in Bolinas, Kyger echoes Whalen's words, as Buddhist practice and writing practice come together for her in a steady, unassuming way: "Zen Buddhism is the practice of sitting meditation, and so is writing. Writing is a practice—it's something that you do every day without thinking about it, whether it's good or bad, and it's just something that you do—you *do* writing" (Grace, "Places to Go").

I have decided to close this essay with a look at "Town Hall Reading with Beat Poets," for in this 1994 poem Kyger regards her literary status with the same wry, self-deprecatory mindset. After appearing on a program with Ed Sanders and other Beat luminaries, Kyger has a moment of enlightenment, a satori:

> Leaving I pick up some trash clogging the exit door.
> It's my book,   *Going On!* What I'm reading from
> tonight, those
> > 'understated Buddhist influenced miniatures'
> > > (says the next day's *NY Times* review)
>
> And it's *my* big dusty footprint on the cover. (*About Now* 593)

Back in the 1970s, Marquette basketball coach Al McGuire liked to place his coffee cup on recruiting letters, so that whenever a ballplayer received a scholarship offer with a big coffee stain on it, he wouldn't get too conceited. Here, Kyger plays a similar joke on herself. Compared to *About Now*, a massive collected poems Kyger published in 2007, *Going On*, published in 1983, is not exactly a doorstopper. But it certainly is a door-clogger, something Kyger had mistaken for trash and stepped upon, leaving on its cover a "big dusty footprint." The poet has left her mark, all right, and it's a Zen riddle, a "Buddhist influenced miniature." There is a lesson here for us all. Why not step on the self the way we occasionally trip over our own two feet? Kyger certainly did, and she wasn't too proud to admit it. Eschewing the ego-gratifying spotlight other Beat poets sought and found, she acceded in her middle and later years to the measured pace of Bolinas, "trying to open/ the path of rhythm with rhythm" (302), taking it day by "grassy bird lit day," realizing quite happily that "we go on, the world/ always goes on, breaking us with its changes/ until our form, exhausted, runs true" (*About Now* 325).

Notes

1. The confluence of Black Mountain and San Francisco Renaissance poets was evident in autumn 1957 as Robert Creeley (with an assist from Allen Ginsberg) edited *Black Mountain Review* #7, which featured a host of Bay Area poets. Kyger saw poets of both groups as she milled about. As Ronna C. Johnson points out, "in summer 1957, the Spicer-Duncan Sunday afternoons devoted to 'lyrically conscious' poetry reached an apex that included John Wieners, George Stanley, James Broughton, Snyder, and Joanne Kyger" ("Mapping Women Writers"). Spicer's *J* magazine was the first outlet to publish a Kyger poem, and it was among a growing list of alternative journals arising in these years. Kyger recalls that Wieners and Joe Dunn were the ones who bestowed upon her the nickname "Miss Kids" when she did poetry readings at The Place, the nickname deriving from her penchant for saying "Hey, kids!" when entering a gathering (Grace, "Places to Go").
2. "The tendency to label this midcentury San Francisco writing as 'Beat' has been an annoying simplification," Kyger announced in a roundtable discussion in 2000. "I never considered myself a Beat writer, nor did the so-called Beat writers of the time consider me one" ("Women and the Beats" 50). A few years earlier, Kyger explained that her "practice of writing was a lot stricter, coming from the energy of Spicer, and someone like Robert Duncan, who was opposed to the tendency of Beat popular poetry writing – to let it all dribble out" (Russo, "Interview").

Kyger revisited Duncan's "scorn" for the Beats in an interview with Nancy M. Grace ("Places to Go"). But a "meta-irony" persisted, Grace suggests, since "Kyger's refusal of any literary affiliation other than self-possession" is, "after all a characteristically Beat stance" ("Places to Go"). In much the same way, it is very Buddhist to deny Buddhahood.

3. The beach itself loosened some restrictions. In a letter he sent in April 1959, Gary Snyder tells Kyger that one of his friends in Japan (Ami Petersen) admired a photograph of Kyger taken at Stinson Beach: "She said you had such a free-feeling look" (Snyder, Letter to Joanne Kyger, April 27, 1959). Snyder is perhaps referring to a photo of Kyger, taken by Tom Field, that is reprinted in David Schneider's recent biography of Philip Whalen (*Crowded* 100), or to another photograph taken on the same beach trip. A year prior, Robert Duncan and Jess Collins decamped to Stinson Beach, viewing the coastal town as a welcome getaway from distractions and controversy swirling in San Francisco Beat culture (Bowles 228-29)

4. The spiritual world is slippery, too, and must be approached the right way. As Snyder would later write, the Dharma is like an avocado: "Hard and slippery/ It looks like/ You should plant it —but then/ It shoots out thru the/ fingers—/ gets away" (*Turtle Island* 61).

5. Journals and notebooks became a key space for Kyger as she meshed natural processes with her own writing process. Andrew Schelling aptly describes Kyger's motivations when composing her journal: "Go out and learn it all: birds, trees, landscapes, people, languages, customs, food, the prices travelers pay and the prices for locals. Get these down while they are close to hand."

6. Brainard assigns a different name to the bush in *Bolinas Journal*: "Joanne and I had fun eating miniature pea pods from Bill's scotch broom tree. And admiring how very noble the eucalyptus trees were (are)" (n.p.).

7. Contrast Brainard's collaborative spirit with Snyder's commentary about Kyger's spontaneous shoreline assemblages. Visiting Ayoya Beach in Japan in August 1960, Kyger and Snyder, along with John Chappell and his wife, "make flower arrangements with driftwood, and each makes their stone garden. After we finish we go around to view them & comment critically. Gary says mine is peaceful but lacks grandeur of vision" (Kyger, *Japan* 46).

8. For more on this poem's hint of impending departure, see Russo, "How You Want," pp. 34-35.

9. Kyger's subconscious invocation of Dharma Rain dates as far back as 1960, during the spring equinox in Japan, when she noted in her journal, "Rain cleans the dirt off all the leaves all day long" (*Japan* 15).

10. Kyger was notable in the New American Poetry movement for refusing self-promotion, Michael Davidson asserts (xiii). Kyger herself admits to being wary of poets assimilated into the academy, finding their "outlaw" status questionable. "The whole occupation of poet, if it does not exist as an entity in the current society, is one that has to do with a spiritual, cultural practice of words, and can't be 'bought.'" (Waldman, "Questions" 127). Alice Notley says that Kyger's exclusion from Paul Hoover's *Postmodern American Poetry* anthology (1994) is due primarily to her reluctance to hew to centers of poetry: "to wield power would be counter to the logic and even the technique of poetry, would be for her a spiritually poor choice" ("Joanne Kyger's Poetry"). In this context, it is not surprising that Kyger once praised Black Mountain College exiles Tom Field and Paul Alexander for not being "self promoters" ("Buzz Time," *There You Are* 33).

Works Cited

Allen, Donald, editor. *The New American Poetry 1945-1960*. 1960. U of California P, 1999.
Bowles, John P. "'Shocking "Beat" Art Displayed': California Artists and the Beat Image." *Reading California: Art, Image, and Identity, 1900-2000*, edited by Stephanie Barron et al., LACMA/U of California P, 2000, pp. 221-46.
Brainard, Joe. *Bolinas Journal*. Big Sky, 1971.
Carden, Mary Paniccia. *Women Writers of the Beat Era: Autobiography and Intertextuality*. U of Virginia P, 2018.
Carolan, Trevor. "Interview with Joanne Kyger" (2007). Kyger, *There You Are*, pp. 25-29.
Creeley, Robert. "A note on Joanne Kyger, June 6, 1988." Kyger, *There You Are,* vii.
---. "Introduction to a Joanne Kyger reading in Buffalo, April 2, 1982." Kyger, *There You Are*, p. 104.
Davidson, Michael. *The San Francisco Renaissance: Poetics and Community at Mid-Century*. 1989. Cambridge UP, 1991.
"Dharma Rain: Lotus Sutra." Translated by Burton Watson. *Dharma Rain: Sources of Buddhist Environmentalism*, edited by Stephanie Kaza and Kenneth Kraft, Shambhala, 2000.
Duberman, Martin. *Black Mountain: An Exploration in Community*. 1972. Northwestern UP, 2009.
Grace, Nancy M., "Places to Go: Interview with Joanne Kyger" (2002). Grace and Johnson, n.p.
Grace, Nancy M., and Ronna C. Johnson, editors. *Breaking the Rule of Cool: Interviewing and Reading Beat Women Writers*. UP of Mississippi, 2004. Accessed as Pro Quest E-book.
Johnson, Ronna C. "Mapping Women Writers." Grace and Johnson, n.p.
Kyger, Joanne. *About Now: Collected Poems*. National Poetry Foundation, 2007.
---. *The Japan and India Journals, 1960-1964*. 1981. Nightboat, 2016.
---. *There You Are: Interviews, Journals, and Ephemera*, edited by Cedar Sigo. Wave, 2017.
McCreary, Chris. "Interview with Joanne Kyger" (2000). Kyger, *There You Are*, pp. 139-42.
Nahem, Lawrence. "Interview with Joanne Kyger" (1974). Kyger, *There You Are*, pp. 65-74.
Notley, Alice. "Joanne Kyger's Poetry." *Arshile: A Magazine of the Arts* 5, 1996, pp. 95-110. Accessed via Electronic Poetry Center, http://writing.upenn.edu.
Russo, Linda. "How You Want to be Styled: Philip Whalen in Correspondence with Joanne Kyger, 1959-1964." *Among Friends: Engendering the Social Site of Poetry*, edited by Anne Dewey and Libbie Rifkin, U of Iowa P, 2013, pp. 21-42.
---. "Interview with Joanne Kyger." *Jacket* 11, Apr. 2000, jacketmagazine.com.

---. "'Precious, rare and mundane': Some Thoughts on the Work of Joanne Kyger." Kyger, *About Now*, pp. 25-29.

Schelling, Andrew. "Joanne Kyger's Portable Poetics." *Jacket* 11, Apr. 2000, jacketmagazine.com.

Schneider, David. *Crowded by Beauty: The Life and Zen of Poet Philip Whalen*. U of California P, 2015.

Smith, Dale. "Energy on the Page: Joanne Kyger in conversation with Dale Smith." *Jacket* 11, Apr. 2000, jacketmagazine.com.

---. "Joanne Kyger and the Narrative of the Everyday." *Jacket* 34, Oct. 2007, jacketmagazine.com.

Smith, Dale, and Michael Price. "Interview with Joanne Kyger" (1997). Kyger, *There You Are*, pp. 105-07.

Snyder, Gary. Letter to Joanne Kyger, April 27, 1959. Gary Snyder Archives, University of California Library, Davis. Used by permission.

---. *Turtle Island*. New Directions, 1974.

Thorpe, John. "Interview with Joanne Kyger" (1983). Kyger, *There You Are*, pp. 97-100.

Vermont, Charlie. "Letter to Linda Russo." *Jacket* 11, Apr. 2000, jacketmagazine.com.

Waldman, Anne. "Questions for Joanne Kyger from Anne Waldman" (2000). Kyger, *There You Are,* pp. 124-28.

Waldman, Anne, and Lewis Warsh, editors. *The Angel Hair Anthology.* Granary, 2001.

"Women and the Beats: Hettie Jones, Joanne Kyger, Janine Pommy Vega, Anne Waldman." *Beats at Naropa: An Anthology*, edited by Anne Waldman and Laura Wright. Coffee House, 2009.

Joanne Kyger's Poetics: Finding the Continuous Thread

Jane Falk

Joanne Kyger's "Artist Statement" for the Foundation for Contemporary Arts emphasizes method while addressing subject matter: "My attention to writing is a daily practice, which then builds an accumulative narrative of chronology. Which ends up as the story of one's life" ("Grants to Artists" para. 1).[1] This essay's emphasis will be on method and a consideration of Kyger's poetics, the continuous thread that runs through her changing and evolving body of work from the 1950s and 1960s and her first published poems through her more experimental work of the 1970s to her later work in *On Time* (2014). Her practice also involves her "lineage" as she terms it in the untitled poem beginning "You know   when you write poetry   you find/ The architecture   of your lineage   your teachers" (1-2).[2] I argue that techniques, methods, and practices Kyger gravitated toward in the 1950s, 1960s, and 1970s inform subsequent poetry and poetics, often demonstrating a connection between her writing as a whole and Buddhist principles.

By poetics, I take for a working definition Andrew Schelling and Anne Waldman in their introduction to *Disembodied Poetics: Annals of the Jack Kerouac School*: "Crafted language. Hence *poetics*—which is the theory and technique of making something out of words" (xii).[3] The *Princeton Encyclopedia of Poetry and Poetics* presents another aspect, that poetics can be derived from poets's "prose statements and from their actual work..." (638). Although Kyger did not make explicitly bold statements similar to Philip Whalen's "Statement on Poetics" ("This poetry is a picture or graph of a mind moving...") for Donald Allen's *The New American Poetry* and was not included in that collection or in *Poetics of The New American Poetry*, where poets were asked to explicate the theoretical underpinnings of their work, statements about her poetics methods can be found throughout her interviews, autobiographical statements, journals, and her poems themselves.[4] For example, in the "Introduction" to *Strange Big Moon*, her Japan and India journals from 1960-64, she notes, "These years also reflect an attempt to investigate the stuff of writing. Is this line any 'good'? How does a poem begin and end" (xi).[5]

Kyger was born in 1934, the daughter of a navy officer. After living in various places, the family settled in Santa Barbara, California, where Kyger attended Santa Barbara College, now University of California–Santa Barbara. She left school one unit short of graduating, moving to San Francisco in 1957 as had her friend Nemi Frost, a painter. Kyger soon became part of the North Beach poetry scene through another painter, Jerome Mallman, who took her to the bar The Place, where former Black Mountain students and teachers hung out. Invited by Joe Dunn and John Wieners, she was soon a regular at the Sunday gatherings led by San Francisco Renaissance poets Jack Spicer and Robert Duncan where she was recognized as a poet after sharing her poem "The Maze" with the group.[6]

Joe Dunn also introduced her to Charles Olson's seminal essay, "Projective Verse," published in *Poetry New York #3*, which had a major influence on the direction of her work, especially her thoughts about the poem as an open form to be filled by the kinetic energy of the poet. She notes in the Dale Smith interview that she read this essay "over and over again, trying to 'fathom' or absorb it. There was a field, an energy, energy on the page. The page itself was an energy source, and words and ideas were transmitted to it" (para. 46). For Olson in "Projective Verse," *kinetics* refers to the energy transferred by the poet via the poem to the reader. Kyger got one of the more important aspects of her poetics from this essay, the importance of the line. Olson's understanding of line length hinges on the breath as an energetic emanation from the body, as he states in "Projective Verse": "And the line comes...from the breath, from the breathing of the man who writes, at the moment that he writes, and thus is, it is here that, the daily work, the WORK, gets in, for only he...can declare, at every moment, the line its metric and its ending—where its breathing, shall come to, termination" (19). The poem then becomes a "FIELD , , , where all the syllables and all the lines must be managed in their relations to each other" (20). Olson's emphasis here on connecting line length physically to the poet's breath would strike a chord with Kyger who was becoming involved in *zazen*, which is Buddhist sitting meditation wherein the practitioner sits silently following his or her breath. In addition, her mentorship with Robert Duncan, who was associated with Olson at Black Mountain College, as well as her friendships with others in San Francisco who had studied there, helped her to incorporate projective verse tenets in her work. For example, Kyger had already begun to break up the line in her early poem "The Maze," especially in the poem's concluding lines.

Joanne Kyger and husband, David Guravich, in Bolinas, c. 2000. Photo Credit: Thomas L. Milligan

This interest in the line in her work would continue in Japan where she lived with then-husband Gary Snyder from 1960-64. Here, Snyder and, indirectly, Kyger were associated with the First Zen Institute of America in Japan. An important aspect of her Japanese stay was Kyger's continued practice of *zazen*. In a 1982 interview with Diana Middleton-McQuaid and John Thorpe, Kyger states of her stay in Japan, "I never learned mantram formally, but I learned about breath, and the long exhalation that develops a diaphragm muscle—which then transfers to the page" (115). The line would be a way to connect writing practice with meditation, and her interest in theorizing the breath line at this time was connected to *zazen* practice. As her line follows her physical breath it also enables a following of the movement of the mind, reflecting what happens in Buddhist meditation. Kyger's comments in her journals from Japan also indicate her search for a more "natural" breath line in poetry. In a journal entry from November 1960, she describes the idea of composing with the tape recorder: "Idea of reading over tape recorder, composing, that is. Playing back and typing it then. The breath line would be natural at least" (*SBM* 62). In taping and playing back her speech, Kyger could ostensibly create a less self-conscious, "natural" breath line, and she could better hear those nuanced breath line pauses that she would carry over into her writing.[7]

During this time, Kyger also read voluminously. Responses to her reading appear in her journals, often in relation to her thoughts on the line.[8] For example, in a January 19, 1963, journal entry, she includes a statement on Pound and imagism from Charles Norman's Pound biography: "'For in the end what differentiates one poet from another is the structure of his line....The poet's line reveals not only his manner of expression, hence the way he thinks; it reveals his intensity—almost it might be said, his way of breathing'" (226-27). Whether Norman had read or heard of Charles Olson is unclear, but Kyger was impressed enough to record the quote in her journal. Similarly to Olson's ideas in "Projective Verse," Norman privileges the "poet's line" (Olson's "breath line") and with it his "intensity" (Olson's "energy"). For both, the poet's line is unique, characteristic, and a key aspect of his or her poetics.[9]

Kyger also used her journals to further experiment with the line, for example, playing with line breaks, which sometimes involved transforming prose texts into poetic ones. She notes of "the 'poems' in the journals, [that] I just considered [them] ways of putting a short lined sketch into the text."[10] For example, on January 2, 1962, with Snyder in Anuradhapura, Ceylon, en route to a meeting in India with Allen Ginsberg and Peter Orlovsky, she transcribed prosaic information from a tombstone or memorial plaque in St. Joseph's church regarding the death of civil servant James Gordon by the "accidental discharge of his gun":

>   This stone
>   Has been placed here
>   by certain members of the public service
>   in memory
>   of a noble action wrought
>   in the year 1868 by
>   JAMES GORDON
>   (*SBM* 154)

Note here not only the moving line, but the echoes of vowel and consonant that carry the reader through the passage. For example, the repetition of vowel sounds in *stone* and *noble* or vowel and consonant sounds in *members* and *memory* provide pattern and rhyme to a free verse text. Kyger was introduced to these techniques by Duncan, who, in turn influenced by Pound, referred to such techniques as the "tone leading of vowels" and "consonant clusters."[11]

What Kyger has done in this passage corresponds with Jonathan Culler's ideas in *Structuralist Poetics*, where he notes, "If one takes a piece of banal journalistic prose and sets it down on a page as a lyric poem, surrounded by intimidating margins of silence, the words remain the same but their effects for readers are substantially altered." He then gives an example from Gerard Genette, adding, "To write this as a poem brings into play a new set of expectations, a set of conventions determining how the sequence is to be read and what kind of interpretations may be derived from it" (161). Kyger, in adjusting the lines of the Gordon text as we might assume she did, adds a sense of greater emphasis and significance to what can seem a somewhat absurd, yet tragic, demise. In the Smith interview, she notes that she saw the page as "some kind of tapestry and voice glyph....The whole movement and rhythm on the page give us instruction as to voice and phrasing and import of what's going on" (para. 30), adding that this is a way of translating "the voice to the page, to get the little subtleties of breath and tone, or change of tone or character emphasis" (para. 34). In comparing the page to a tapestry, Kyger suggests the way her line breaks present an interwoven whole. The term *glyph* refers generally to a symbol that conveys information nonverbally.[12] Hence, Kyger's use of capitalization, as well as spacings and line breaks, create visual patterns on the page and can score the poem for the poet—or any reader, for that continued matter.

Concerns with the line on her return to the United States, where Kyger put these ideas and methods into practice as she readied her first book of poems *The Tapestry and the Web* (1965) for publication by Donald Allen and his Four Seasons Foundation. In a 1974 interview with Robert Bertholf, she remembers that in writing and structuring the Odyssey Poems, the last seven poems of this book, "I really diagrammed them....I put a straight line down the middle and made everything branch off like a tree. It had its roots on the ground and then things branch off from either side of it. You could fit all the voices and patterns that got into the movement that way" (65).[13] In "Projective Verse," Olson explicates such line movement as the "progressing" and "backing up" of the "meaning" and "movement" of the poem. For Kyger, these moving lines help present the unfolding of the narrative, as well as a way to present shifts in speaker, point of view, or scene.

The play of the line and line breaths would become an important constant throughout Kyger's writing career, as her experiments with lineation demonstrate. During the Bertholf interview she claims to be more interested in the paragraph as form, but the importance of breath remains: "Yes, I'm into the paragraph a lot now, because it gives me a sense of continuity....I guess I get tired of the lines. A paragraph is a big breath..." (66). She also notes the power of the short epigrammatic line: "You can go back into that one line and it will keep giving off overtones..." (65).

Similarly in an interview this same year with Lawrence Nahem she states that "a word reverberates," adding, "As long as it'll reverberate and keep doing that vibration of meaning, then it works. I really like phrases now that have some internal turning, that seem to turn around all the time inside" (155). In a journal entry of February 1, 1963, Kyger explicates *turning*: "Suggest and suggest and keep *turning*. Slightest hint only to follow the turn. The surprise is innocence and revelation of the mind" (*SBM* 230). Stan Persky, another poet in the Duncan/Spicer circle, posits that "turn" had to do with "our version of 'enjambment.'" The turning word or line can be a "pivot for two different stories."[14] Thus Kyger's idea of turning enabled her to create subtle and unexpected shifts in a poem's meaning (the element of "surprise" for readers). These variations on the breath line are evident in poems published in her 1970 collections, *Places To Go* and *Joanne*.

Both of those works demonstrate another important aspect of her practice at the time, poems conceived as a series, her introduction to which was through Duncan and Spicer. According to his Preface to *Medieval Scenes*, Duncan was the first of the San Francisco Renaissance poets to write a serial poem. In the spring of 1947, he "proposed the ten nightly sessions in which I wrote *Medieval Scenes*," adding that "for Spicer *Medieval Scenes* was the initial spectacle of the dictated poem and of the serial poem..." (n.p.). Spicer describes the serial poem in the first of his Vancouver Lectures of 1965: "When I'm writing a poem, I always try not to see the connections" (23). In the second lecture he explains that "you go from one point to another to another to another, not really knowing where you are from point A to point B" (73).[15] Spicer's admonition to "try to keep as much of yourself as possible out of the poem" relates to the dictated nature of such poems and the fact that they come from "Outside" the poet (8).[16]

Kyger was exposed to these ideas about writing serial poems when she attended Duncan and Spicer's Sunday afternoon poetry group. In Lew Ellingham's 1982 interview with Kyger and Ebbe Borregaard, Ellingham asks Kyger whether *The Tapestry and the Web* was a serial poem.[17] Answering in the negative, she first describes serial poems as "not one long poem," adding that "once you start writing you can do that over a period of time, like, every day..." (107). She elaborates on this idea, noting that "you write one poem, then you write another poem the next day that relates to the poem before so you're addressing yourself as a dialogue that goes on..." (109). Her ideas about serial poems here reflect the practice of both Duncan and Spicer and provided a new direction for her poetry. Poems in *The Tapestry and the Web* were thematically related, according to Kyger, whereas serial poems appear in her second book, *Places To Go*.

Serial poems in this volume such as "Places To Go," "The Test of Fantasy," "A Novel," or "Poems from Rome," most in paragraph form, date from 1966-67, written during a year when Kyger and her then-husband Jack Boyce, a painter, travelled to Europe and New York. Even though some of these poems appear to have autobiographical aspects—especially the six-part "Places To Go," which mentions a sister, mother, Daddy, grandmother, and aunt in various situations and relationships—the shifts in point of view, as well as the juxtapositions of place and situation and lack of narrative continuity, give a surrealistic quality to domesticity. In addition, many individual sentences are ambiguous with a heavy use of pronouns missing antecedents or context, confusing any autobiographical effect. For example, Kyger described the eight-chapter "A Novel" as "a mixture of dream continuity and everyday happenings, with some Tibetan tantra tanka's, which I have just seen, mixed in" ("Joanne Kyger" 199).[18] The poem begins with the lines "I woke up very angry because I wanted to see where they/ were and I couldn't see where they were" (1-2). No context or antecedents are provided for these pronouns in Chapter One, and other chapters do not continue this narrative.

"The Test of Fantasy" is a more complex eight-part series wherein the speaker presents similar stream of consciousness impressions in interior and exterior spaces, while contemplating the writing of a serial poem in light of Spicer's directives that poems be dictated from "Outside." Kyger commented on the formal aspects of this poem ("a continuous narrative sort") in a 1969 letter to George Quasha, editor of the magazine *Stony Brook*: "The movement of space the poem usually covers on the physical page, has been simplified to ordinary margin to margin lines, so that the mind or head is allowed to trip unimpeded in a new progression."[19] These comments follow her linear experiments in the Odyssey poems, but precede comments to Bertholf on her interest in paragraph form. The paragraph form is a less artificial presentation of line breaks and the way most "ordinary" reading is done. Here the line follows the mind in a "new progression" (new for Kyger) and one that differs sharply from the stepped and branching lines of *The Tapestry and the Web*.

In each section, aspects of writing a serial poem are discussed, seemingly in dialogue with each other and with the poem's speaker, who is engaged in the activities of daily life. The first section concludes with a comment on how the poem should be conceived: "Selfless—that was the proposition" (12), following Spicer's directive to keep "yourself" out of the poem. In the second section, the speaker notes that "she used various modes of expression that/ were current" (2.4-5), asking in the section's tenth paragraph, "Why *not* fantasy?" (2.31). The third section begins, "I'm glad to get back," as the poem's speaker gets back to writing the serial poem. The section ends with another rejection of the self: "Lost under the weight/ of the garbage of who are you that you are not making apparent" (3.24-25). However, this must be done speedily and spontaneously: "Not costumes, or paraphernalia, the immediate reactions" should make up the dictated poem (3.27). Spicer's comment that he tries not to see connections between serial poems is relevant here. For Kyger this is done without intellectualizing or, as she writes, putting "costumes" on the persona. In the fourth section, the speaker complains, "The form is no/ longer obvious to me" (4.8-9), while in the fifth, the speaker remembers a woman who grew older without models: "There wasn't any model except the one she built,/ and one could scarcely believe there was no established pattern" (5.16-17). Writing practice is implied, perhaps referring to the spontaneous quality of dictated poetry. In the sixth section, the first paragraph ends with the quandary, "There isn't any message to be spoken," while the entire section concludes more optimistically that the speaker "noted the elegant turns, the/ twisting statements grooving into the language building something/ to listen to" (6.17-19). Here the run-on effect mirrors Spicer's suggestion in the Vancouver lectures to go from point to point to point not really knowing where you are. The seventh section begins, "I am sure my dreams must have been of the wrong sort," as the speaker again doubts the process. In the eighth and concluding section the speaker contemplates aspects of writing such as energy, stories, and character, with the section and poem ending as follows: "Memory has its own screen across the room to view/ itself, and the continuous dwelling of conjecture takes permanent form/ in stiff-legged walks to remind, thus on and on the breathing goes" (8.54-56). The dictation has stopped and only the breathing continues. Here Kyger ties in Duncan and Spicer's ideas that the serial poem is dictated and comes from Outside the poet with Olson's breath line and overtones of Buddhist *zazen* sitting meditation.

In contrast, *Joanne* is made up of fairly short "epigrammatic" lines, which at times create haiku-like poems with some degree of humor and ambiguity. Of the 37 poems, 24 are under six lines in length. The untitled poems obliquely describe the speaker's life, presenting self-reflections during one summer in Bolinas with friends at home and at the beach, characterized on the book's back cover as a novel "from the inside out." Thus the book opposes dualities of inside and out, a way for Kyger to deal with opposites and to overcome duality, which are both Buddhist goals.[20] D.T. Suzuki discusses the overcoming of opposites in the first series of his essays on Zen Buddhism in "Practical Methods of Zen Instruction." He also emphasizes the fact that "Zen mistrusts the intellect, does not rely upon traditional and dualistic methods of reasoning, and handles problems after its own original manners" (270-71).[21] Kyger had been struggling to overcome the intellect since a March 1963 journal entry: "There should be no artificial abbreviations...in poetry. Closer to the mind it comes out how? Or the mind closer to the poem, comes out with its own good poetry" (*SBM* 242). In other words, the poem should be an attempt to directly transcribe the experiences of daily life, somewhat like a journal entry, without separation between mind and poem, *Joanne* being such a series of poems.

Kyger demonstrates the serial effect as well as the juxtaposition of opposites in these poems, for example syntactic juxtaposition in a poem of two lines: "Some thing open/ Some thing closed." Here, the use of the indefinite pronoun *thing* leaves the reader with an ambiguous feeling and without the closure of specificity. This poem also relates to Kyger's journal entry from March 1960, which states, "I am neither open nor closed/ a/ leaky faucet" (*SBM* 13). The book's penultimate poem of three lines also plays with oppositions as well as ambiguity, while approaching the form of the Japanese haiku: "a life time/ what happened/ it stopped." Opposite processes are juxtaposed, suggesting the idea of death, although the pronoun *it*, with its indefinite signification, leaves such an allusion questionable. Ambiguity is also evident in the way the second line can be read as question or statement. Haiku is suggested, although the jump in thought occurs between the first and second lines rather than between second and third as in traditional haiku. In the final poem of *Joanne,* Kyger again uses the pronoun *it* to respond to the previous poem, to create ambiguity, as well as to demonstrate complementary and oppositional aspects: "It's always free/ It's always easy" (1-2). Again, there is the suggestion of death, always free, not always easy. The two almost identical lines have only one differing word each, but even these words have similar vowel sounds and so echo each other without being opposite or identical states. Here sound connects to reinforce sense and recalls the experiments in turning prose to poetry in the epitaph for James Gordon.[22]

Instead of reading *Joanne* and serial poems in *Places To Go* as the discourse of a subject *I* who moves through space in Europe or Bolinas, California, one could also read them as examples of the Russian Formalist Viktor Shklovskii's concept of *ostranenie*, or defamiliarization. Nina Kolesnikoff in the *Encyclopedia of Contemporary Literary Theory* notes that according to Shklovskii, "The meaning of art is based on the ability to 'defamiliarize' things, to show them in a new, unexpected way....Art 'defamiliarizes' objects by making forms strange, and by increasing the difficulty and the length of perception..." (528). In "The Test of Fantasy," which I have suggested is a serial poem ultimately about the writing of serial poems, there are at times unclear connections between paragraphs or between sections, despite the fact that there are recurring characters providing some sense of continuity. In the case of *Joanne*, readers are not always sure as to where or when an action occurs, and there are few specific descriptions of the *I* who inhabits the poems. Abrupt juxtapositions between lines, paragraphs, and poems contribute to the defamiliarizing effect.[23]

Although Kyger seems to have stopped writing such explicit types of serial poems with *Places To Go* and *Joanne*, one might consider her dated poems of daily life as a continuation of the impetus to seriality in her work. Kyger created entire books made up of such poems, for example, *The Wonderful Focus of You* (1980). In many cases, one dated entry or poem responds to a previous one, reflecting Spicer and Duncan's ideas about the serial poem. The way that poems in a series respond to each other is more obvious in longer poems made up of shorter ones, covering shorter periods of time. For example, "Living a Spiritual Life in the 'Woods'" is made up of a series of eight short poems from October 2 to 8, 1998, a response to "Some Choice," Kyger's poem describing a critique of her lifestyle in the periodical *Gare du Nord*. Such a technique can also be seen in her last major collection *On Time*, in which the series of nine poems titled "Dreaming Poets in Mexico with the *I Ching,* a Oaxaca Notebook October 2011," date from October 4 to 18. Here one entry is in dialogue with the next and with the inhabitants of Oaxaca, statements by American politician Rick Perry, poets she dreams about such as Olson and Ginsberg, the I Ching and her own self-reflections and observations.

The way "Dreaming Poets in Mexico with the *I Ching*" includes such a wide variety of texts demonstrates open form, another important aspect of Kyger's poetics.[24]

Kyger may first have become aware of this technique when she read William Carlos Williams's *Paterson*, as she writes in the 1992 Gale autobiographical statement that *Paterson* Book V made a "great impression." She adds, quoting herself, possibly from a journal entry of the time, "'He allows the poem to contain so much, letters, quotations, poetry of others, and it works so beautifully!'" (192). In a similar way, Kyger's work, both poems and published journals, often contain such a variety of texts and enable her to break the limits of the lyric poem.

For Kyger, an interest in the journal as a publishable genre directly relates to her interest in open form. In the interview with Tyler Doherty and Tom Morgan on what they call "poetic journals," Kyger states of the journal as genre: "I consider it a completely free and open form, anything and everything can go onto the pages" (136).[25] This interest in recording daily life in the present moment also reflects the Buddhist idea of *tathata* or suchness, which Suzuki in his 1958 essay in *Evergreen*, "Aspects of Japanese Culture," defines as the "world of particulars" (54).[26] An early inspiration for journals as a publishable genre was the binding of her Japanese notebooks by Snyder before she left Japan. She remarks on the way their binding gave them the character of a published book, while acknowledging Snyder's daily journal practice as inspirational.[27] Others such as Snyder and Ginsberg had also published journals; it was reasonable for Kyger to want to do likewise.[28]

However, Kyger's Japanese and Indian journals were not her first journal publication, an honor that goes instead to *Desecheo Notebook* (1971). Wesley Tanner of Arif Press explains that he had heard Kyger read and asked her for a manuscript to publish.[29] The only one she had ready at the time was her notebook from a trip to Desecheo Island with Peter Warshall, which became *Desecheo Notebook*.[30] Similar to other of her published journals, *Desecheo Notebook* is an open form containing a variety of material such as dreams (printed in block format), diary-like observations of daily life, and poems. In the interview with Doherty and Morgan she notes of the journal that "for me it means a kind of movement back and forth from prose-like descriptive narrative bridges into shorter poem-like lines....And the element of time, happening in the moment, aware of the moment" (137). In *Desecheo Notebook*, the entries present such a movement between inner and outer worlds, between kinds of human interaction, and between writing and life. The way that the entries move from thought to observation to dream and back may demonstrate the Buddhist theories of Net of Indra (*pratitya samutpada*), the idea that all entities are interconnected and interdependent, as these parts of her world are likewise, and as her poems and journals express.

Kyger provides additional insights into her use of journals, especially as sources for poems, in an interview with poet Anne Waldman in 2000: "I always begin with the date and the time. This is a moment of entering into history, and however one writes, one *is* writing one's history. One day happens after another" (293). Here journal writing approaches the serial as well as the autobiographical. Kyger then describes how she uses her journals as sources for poems, using as example her book *Patzcuaro* (1999), written on a visit to Mexico from 1997-98. Noting that on a previous visit "not a lot of 'poems' arrived," she wanted to try again: "I approached this formally at a certain time every day, and excerpted journal entries I had written over the past weeks....I did this periodically over our forty-day stay and the poems in the book resulted" (289).[31] An examination of the poems in this book shows open form in Kyger's use of a variety of texts such as self-reflections, lists of objects, dreams, the history of Patzcuaro, headlines of the moment, and found text from the memoirs of Pablo Neruda.

An important aspect of open form is the inclusion of dreams in her work. As early as the 1960s, Kyger was interested in dreams, as she notes in a journal entry of March 5, 1960, in *Strange Big Moon*: "Jumps in thought that Persky's Sappho poem takes are beautiful. And make that sort of *joining* — implies a logic that moves beneath like the logic of dream..." (30).[32] Kyger has also stated that "dreams were... an important part of the so called Beat writers careful morning records."[33] As well as including dreams in published journals, Kyger uses dreams in her poems, as her discussion with Chris McCreary in 2000 demonstrates: "I use dreams of the night before all the time to start off a piece of writing and often don't make any distinction between the dream and what is going on at the moment of writing in the 'real' awake world" (140). The seamless movement from dream to reality often provides a surreal quality to Kyger's work that is most evident in the serial poems in *Places To Go*. Again, this is an example of defamiliarization, which may also create a kind of *satori* or awakening effect in the reader.

Dreams relate to Buddhist philosophy in another way, through the understanding that the dream world and the "'real' awake world" are basically the same, both ultimately empty. According to Herbert Guenther's translation of *The Life and Teaching of Naropa*, which Kyger used as the basis for a series of her poems, "Life of Naropa," "Both Sutras and Mantra texts assert that the whole of entitative reality is like a dream....Therefore for undermining the belief in the exclusive reality of what appears during daytime, the fact of dreaming is the most excellent index...as to the illusory-hallucinatory nature of our world" (67-68).[34] In other words, the dream is as real as waking daily life for Buddhism, which considers life to be a dream, and each person needs to wake up to the dream that is life, as well as the life that is dream.

Kyger's use and inclusion of the texts of others as in "Life of Naropa" is yet another aspect of open form in her work. For example, her practice of reading/writing through texts is evident in *Some Sketches from the Life of Helena Petrovna Blavatsky*, "Descartes and the Splendor Of," "Up My Coast," and "The Beautiful Adjectives and Magnificent Metaphors of Pablo Neruda."[35] Kyger attributes her methodology here to the influence of a lecture Ed Sanders gave at Naropa in 1977 on what he calls Investigative Poetry.[36] Sanders's Investigative Poetry necessitates collecting historical data of all kinds: opening case files, drawing graphs, and creating grids and collages. He recommends using "*every* bardic skill and meter and method of the last 5 or 6 generations, in order to describe *every* aspect...of the historical present..." (11). He quotes Olson frequently throughout, citing the importance of his

Maximus poems, as well as Pound's Cantos and Ginsberg's "Howl." In the Smith interview, Kyger remembers the immediate impact of these concepts: "I thought the role of the historical investigator was a great one for the poet. It gave them something to do, other than ramble on about their feelings and nature. One could open up the 'past' and the writers one felt an affinity with..." (para. 6), agreeing with his comment that she used this method with the Blavatsky book. This is a way for Kyger to avoid the confessional mode and bring texts she deems important to the attention of her readers.

However, a comparison of Kyger's method of investigative poetry with that of Sanders's presents more differences than similarities. She works primarily with the texts of others, summarizing, condensing, and excerpting passages, sometimes using exact quotations indicated by quotation marks, sometimes closely paraphrasing. For example, Kyger's *Sketches From the Life of Helena Petrovna Blavatsky* condenses Sylvia Cranston's 411-page biography of Madame Blavatsky, 19th century co-founder of the Theosophical Society, into an approximately 20-page long poem or "bio-sketch" of 11 sketches that at times directly quote or closely paraphrase from what might be considered an appropriated text. Beginning with Mme. Blavatsky's birth and ending with her death, Kyger includes highlights of her life in between, such as her meeting with Colonel Henry Steel Olcott with whom she founded the Theosophical Society. However, a good part of one of the 11 sketches is devoted to Blavatsky's comments on the deforestation of India. Here, Kyger highlights information she deems essential, but which is not a major aspect of Blavatsky's life, taking up only half a page of the 411-page biography. Kyger's major innovation in this work is to change a prose text into a poetic one, returning to the experiments with translating prose into poetry that she had begun in 1962 with the epitaph of James Gordon.[37]

In addition, Kyger had been using the texts of others as the basis for her own work and as ways to implement open form long before she heard Sanders's lecture. An important example is her 1968 poem "Descartes and the Splendor Of" based on philosopher Rene Descartes's *Discourse on Method*. The six-part poem published in *Places To Go* was used as the script for her 1968 video, *Descartes*, in which she plays the French philosopher. Here again, she brings closely paraphrased or directly quoted material from Descartes into her own text, often using capitalization to indicate direct quotation. Although in her Gale autobiographical statement she calls this "an 11-minute translation" of Descartes (200), it is more of a revision. Not only does she impersonate Descartes in her video, but from the fourth part to the end of the poem/script, she feminizes Descartes's masculine God, where his *God* becomes her *Mother God*. The first such rewriting occurs in Descartes's discussion of the idea of perfection, which he writes had been placed in him "by a Nature which was really more perfect than mine . . . which even had within itself all the perfections of which I could form any idea — that is to say . . . In a word, which was God" (102). Kyger's version is almost the same but for the last word: "PLACED IN ME BY A NATURE...

WHICH EVEN POSSESSES WITHIN ITSELF ALL THE PERFECTION OF WHICH I COULD FORM ANY IDEA, that is to say IN A SINGLE WORD, *MOTHER GOD*" (4.20-23, caps in original). The substitution of feminine for masculine continues throughout the last three parts, augmented by Kyger's acting and dramatic tones of voice. Kyger gets the last word here as she adds her coda to the discourse: "Mother God in the Castle of Heaven" (6.19).[38] Several years after her video experience, she commented in the Nahem interview that poetry is "storytelling, and it's acting and it is music too and it's theatre" (146). Thus the video work with emphasis on voice and tone in action before an audience would reinforce not only Kyger's interests in the page as a score for her voice, but also poetry as a multimedia experience.

Then too, open form relates to Kyger's attitude toward revision, which she claimed she did not practice. She may delete, but she does not rewrite, as she notes in the "Introduction" to *Strange Big Moon*: "These journals were never rewritten or polished up for publication" (xi). She corroborates this in the Smith interview: "You can tidy up a bit, but often you lose the breath and flow of the minute when you re-write" (para. 24). She may have been influenced here by San Francisco Renaissance poets, as she remembers Sunday afternoons with Spicer and Duncan, and "disagreements about writing, 'you can't rewrite a poem...'" (Ellingham interview 99).[39] This is despite her 2013 poem from *On Time*, "Stoutly Maintains I Never Rewrite," which begins,

> So what about those many sheets of drifting time
>   and intents
>   hoping to "pin down"
> the illusive tone
> that makes a poem (1-5)

These opening lines seem to belie the poem's title, as the "many sheets" of time imply the many sheets of paper used to "'pin down'" a poem. Here Kyger appears to call herself out. Perhaps she did revise at times.

Similar to her comments on revision, Kyger provided numerous statements about what one might consider her poetic practices, while also contradicting or distancing herself from such intellectualizing or theorizing. In the Nahem interview, for example, she notes that her "feeling about what the poem is has changed a lot. I write things down...and then there's the decision as to how is that in poetry" (154). In being asked how her "sense of the poem has changed," she observes that "I used to think of it as having more of a form. Like you sit down and write a poem—but this isn't poetry, this is prose, or this is not a poem, why isn't this a poem. And now I think almost anything that a poet wants to call a poem is a poem" (155).[40] These comments recall her move from the lineation in *The Tapestry and the Web* to experiments with paragraph form in *Places To Go*.

More recently, in a 2011 poem from *On Time*, "'Write Something About Poetics,'" a title possibly inspired by a request from an eager researcher, she neatly sidestepped the directive. Instead the poem is a meditation on change, beginning with a dream of the past and memories of a 1970 poetry reading, followed by questions of an existential or Buddhist nature: "Where did/ all those late night thoughts go?/ About Emptiness" (8-10). The speaker then states a preference for "mature" vs. "old" as a way to describe herself, and then concludes with a haiku-like observation watching "the great Blue/ Heron strike a gopher in its hole/ and gulp it down" (18-20). The poem demonstrates the processes and materiality of her poetics, specifically her use of dreams, memories, and observations from nature directly recorded in the moment's immediacy. For Kyger, writing is a process and a practice, not to be intellectualized.

Despite such resistance to the theoretical, her many statements about the way she writes provide a rich trove of ideas and favored poetic methods and techniques: linear play, the serial poem, open form, and appropriation of the texts of others. It is obvious from looking at the various constants of her poems and practice over time that a continuous thread exists in the formal aspects of her work. Her serial poems of daily life and her use of journals as open form emphasize writing as daily practice. The most significant of these practices and most central over time can be considered the line that furnishes the "architecture of the page," along with the open form that allows a variety of texts and techniques to enter the poem. Shifts in Kyger's style often hinge on what she thinks about the line, until a time in her writing career when one might consider that a mature style takes hold. Even then, there remain numerous variations, primarily in the way she deploys the line. Late poems demonstrate such techniques, especially the deployment of the breath line with vowel and consonant repetitions, which she refers to as tonal bridging in the 1997 poem, "A violin plays a sprightly 10 note theme," where "the violin theme so sweetly played/ with space between, no need to make a narrative or/ tonal bridge" (9-11). Line breaks act as thought breaks, giving a surreal quality to the work. In addition, open form journals create wholes out of diverse types of texts, leaving readers to create meaning. Defamiliarization also occurs in Kyger's use of found texts, where readers are not always sure which words are Kyger's and which those of the text she has appropriated, or even what text she is incorporating and making her own.

Buddhist teachings play a part, as well. Although she notes in *Lo and Behold* (2009) that Buddhism affects her writing "Very conscious little," the specifics that follow seem to belie her words: "Attempt to erase 'I' or make it very translucent. Depicting states of mind as ephemeral, but lots of fun. The common ordinary voice" (24).[41] Kyger makes an important point about Buddhism and poetry in a 1998 interview with David Meltzer, noting the way that following the breath in meditation is similar to the way thoughts arise in the poetic process: "So what arises comes out. And then the next thing arises, and so you put that down" (129). Compare this with Olson's similar ideas in "Projective Verse" that "ONE PERCEPTION MUST IMMEDIATELY AND DIRECTLY LEAD TO A FURTHER PERCEPTION" (17, caps in original). Here Olson suggests a shift in subject matter, "getting rid of the lyrical interference of the individual as ego, of the '-subject'" (24). This loss of ego intersects nicely with Buddhist tenets. Other important Buddhist aspects in Kyger's poetry include the importance of the quotidian, her interest in dreams, the attempt to overcome duality, and the idea of interrelatedness. It is not so much that Kyger consciously espouses Buddhism as that her practices align with such tenets, perhaps because of her Buddhist practice over the years. Kyger's example provides another link between Buddhism and the Beat avant-garde in the 1950s and 1960s, as part of the turn to alternatives to Western spiritual and philosophical ideas after World War II.

Another important thread through Kyger's work relates to her lineage and debt thereunto. Most significant teachers appear to be theorists such as Williams and Olson, and the poets of the San Francisco Renaissance, Spicer and Duncan. In the Middleton-McQuaid and Thorpe interview regarding Spicer and Duncan, Kyger notes that "Robert Duncan had a lot more compassion for allowances in writing, but he would go home at night and Spicer would be the one who would be drinking with you..." (112). Beat writers appear less often in this chronology, as comrades in poetic arms, contemporaries who provide encouragement, example, and even rivalry: in the poem, "You know when you write poetry," they are "Beats which gave confidence/ and competition" (4-5).[42] Specifically, note the teaching aspect of Whalen in his letters to her suggesting books she should read, as well as the writing practices of Whalen, Welch, and Snyder, among others, which she observed first hand during her stay at East-West House and later in her Japan and India years. However, early in her writing career, she moved from Muse to poet with the help of her journal, working it out for herself.

Just as Kyger used the ideas of her contemporaries and teachers as influences for her own theories, so she also adapted them to her own needs, as she adapted Olson's breath line to the paragraph form in the 1970s, or the serial form for her poems of daily life in Bolinas, one poem following or responding to the next, "all this every day" and "again," as her titles remind readers. Thus, though there is continuity over time (a continuous thread), there is also variation (change and flow to the process).[43] She dwells in practice more than product. Barrett Watten's description of poetics in his Introduction to *A Guide to Poetics Journal* illuminates our understanding of Kyger in this regard. He describes the "fields of meaning" of poetics and "the manner in which the work of art extends its principles of construction, the way it makes meaning, through the contexts it draws from, finally, to transform them" (11). Just so, Kyger adopted and transformed a mid-20th century poetics to the needs of her poetry situated in its own time and place.

Notes

1. Kyger received the grant for poetry in 2005-06 from this foundation. She has made similar statements about the autobiographical nature of her work, for example, in her interview with Nancy M. Grace. Such a narrative does not involve the confessional poem; note her distaste for this mode in this interview.
2. In the 1997 Dale Smith interview, she defines this as "who your teachers are, how did you learn the architecture of your page, become aware of the 'structure' of your thinking and the books in your life" (para. 70).
3. Kyger taught at Naropa from 1976-2015. She first went there in 1975 to give a reading, as she explains in her interview with John Whalen-Bridge, "Poetry and Practice at Naropa University."
4. Whalen's statement also appears as "Since You Ask Me" in *Memoirs of an Interglacial Age*. Kyger was included in a version of *The New American Poetry* entitled *The New Writing in the USA* (1967), edited by Donald Allen and Robert Creeley, published only in the U.K.
5. These journals are hereafter referred to as *SBM*, a 2000 reprint of *The Japan and India Journals* originally published by Tombouctou Press in 1981. There is also a 2016 edition titled *The Japan and India Journals*.
6. This autobiographical information is from her statement for Gale *Contemporary Authors*. Kyger was one of the few women accepted as a poet by this group. See Linda Russo's interview with Kyger for more on her relationship with Duncan and Spicer.
7. Ronna C. Johnson uses this quote to note Kyger's "technology of breath poetics" in her essay on Beat poetics (85).
8. Primary sources of books for Kyger were the British and American cultural libraries, as she explains in the 2007 Tyler Doherty and Tom Morgan interview (135). As well, she was influenced by materials friends sent from the U.S.
9. Earlier in the book, Norman quotes Pound himself on the line as "a perfect test of his [the poet's] natural vigor and of his poetic nature" (40).
10. Quote from "Jane Falk Questions" (2010), unpaginated.
11. Kyger describes Duncan's class in "The Dharma Committee" as "more talk about vowels and consonants" (381). This journal written in 1958 is reprinted in Kyger's collected poems, *About Now*. Duncan appears to have been influenced by Ezra Pound's "Cleaner's Manifesto," sent from St. Elizabeth's in 1948 where he had been incarcerated after World War II. As Duncan writes in his essay "Projective Project: Charles Olson," "The three things from Pound were to 'follow the tone leading of vowels...to watch the consonant clusters...to debunk by lucidity'" (35).
12. More specifically, *glyph* recalls Olson's interest in Mayan culture. He states in *Mayan Letters* that the glyph was a form which "unfolded directly from content" (68), one of the principles of Projective Verse. The exact quote from "Projective Verse" is "FORM IS NEVER MORE THAN AN EXTENSION OF CONTENT" (16, caps in original). Kyger mentions reading *Mayan Letters* during her stay in Mexico in *Phenomenological* (1989).
13. Most of these poems first appeared in *Open Space*, a journal published over the course of 1965, which was masterminded by Jack Spicer and edited by Stan Persky.
14. This quote is from an email to this author January 28, 2018. The idea of turning may have come from Duncan, who associates it with the projective in "Projective Project," that "we see this object and we turn it around...we describe it in all its ways..." (33).
15. These lectures are published in *The House That Jack Built*.
16. The idea of keeping "yourself" out of the poem would also resonate with Kyger, as it echoes Buddhism's ideas about ego and the realization that, according to D.T. Suzuki, there is "no ego-substance behind our mental life" (*Essays, 1st Series* 58).
17. The interview was research for the Spicer study *Poet Be Like God*.

18. This may be the novel she refers to in "Letter from Paris" (1966), in which she states that "we're writing novels just like everybody else" (44). This poem is titled "A Novel in Paris" in *About Now*.
19. This correspondence is in conjunction with the publication of Kyger's poem in Quasha's magazine *Stony Brook* ¾. Per Quasha, correspondence was probably initiated by Gary Snyder. Note that this poem, "A Test of Fantasy," was originally published as one continuous text; it was later published in *Places To Go* as "The Test of Fantasy" in eight parts. Quoting from this letter is courtesy of the Estate of Joanne Kyger and Special Collections and Archives University of California, San Diego Library.
20. Suzuki addresses this specifically in "Philosophy of the Prajnaparamita" from his 3rd series of essays as "reversing the order of one's mental outlook. What used to be dualistic is now to be seen from the 'wrong side' of it. The inside which was hitherto hidden out of sight now stands revealed in full view" (273).
21. In numerous interviews—with David Meltzer, for example—Kyger notes her familiarity with Suzuki's writings.
22. Duncan writes in "Projective Project" that when tuning in on vowel sounds "you'll still have rhymes, which make very strange sense. That's one of their great advantages..." (35).
23. The presence of the Language Poets in the Bay Area in the 1970s and their interest in Russian Formalism may be relevant here. Some of this group had connections with Bolinas; Kyger wrote several poems to Language Poet Robert Grenier, for example.
24. Olson equates open verse with projective verse and composition by field. Duncan also emphasizes the open aspect of Olson's Projective Verse in "Projective Project," citing Olson's use of history, including footnotes (40).
25. Here Kyger goes on to list all her publications that she considers to be journals: *Desecheo Notebook, Trip Out and Fall Back, Visit to Maya Land, Phenomenological, Wonderful Focus of You,* and *The Dharma Committee*.
26. Here, recall William Carlos Williams's poetics "no ideas but in things."
27. Statement from July 15, 2002, interview with the author.
28. For more on Beats and journal as genre see Falk, "Journal as Genre and Published Text: Beat Avant-Garde Writing Practices."
29. See Falk, "Journal as Genre and Published Text." Tanner noted that he published the journal without much editing.
30. Desecheo Island is off the coast of Puerto Rico; Warshall was there on a scientific expedition.
31. The idea from Spicer's dictation—that a poem happens to or arrives in a poet's mind from Outside—is relevant here.
32. In this untitled poem beginning with the line "the thing that is beautiful in me &," Persky begins with the idea of beauty and a quote from Robert Creeley, then moves rapidly from orchard to bar, to flowers in a doorway, Kyger's house, Greece and California, before ending with an image of Sappho. The poem is courtesy of the author and Special Collections and Archives, University of California, San Diego Library.
33. Statement from "Jane Falk Questions" (2010), unpaginated.
34. Also note her allusion to the Taoist Chuang Tzu's parable, which asks, "AM I A BUTTERFLY DREAMING I AM ME or ME DREAMING I AM A BUTTERFLY," in her 1968 poem "Descartes and the Splendor Of."
35. She also uses found quotes as the titles of poems, which often enables ironic commentary or response to the quote. For example, "'Are You One of those Revolutionary Poets?'" from *On Time* is perhaps the question of a researcher, with the quotes around the title reinforcing this idea.
36. Sanders's book by that title was published by City Lights Books in 1976.
37. This is where Sanders and Kyger do meet in their mutual interest in open form and experimental composition.

38. "Descartes and the Splendor Of" also provides examples of the way that Kyger substituted key words in a text for her more conversational or slangy version, or to introduce Buddhist terminology. While Descartes reflects upon the "fact that I doubted and that consequently my existence was not perfect" (105), Kyger expressed this as "I realize that to doubt is a drag" (102).
39. Note here similarities with other Beat Generation poets on revision.
40. This is similar to Marcel Duchamp's creation and championing of the readymade; even a manufactured object is art if an artist deems it so.
41. This work is a composite from 1980-1992 notebooks.
42. Here see Linda Russo on Kyger and Whalen and the *Occident* interview, in which Kyger lists many poets she regards as her teachers.
43. Perhaps not enough has been said about Kyger's conversational and humorous voice and tone, illusive poetic qualities of which Kyger is a master; these are perhaps more dependent on content and word choice than on the way the words are laid out on the page, or more a matter of content than form. However, I have tried to avoid pitting form against content, a false dichotomy, keeping in mind Robert Creeley's dictum that form is an extension of content.

Works Cited

Cranston, Sylvia. *HPB: The Extraordinary Life and Influence of Helena Blavatsky, Founder of The Modern Theosophical Movement.* G.P. Putnam's Sons, 1993.

Culler, Jonathan. *Structuralist Poetics.* Cornell UP, 1975.

Descartes, Rene. *The Philosophical Works of Descartes.* Translated by Elizabeth S. Haldane and G.R.T. Ross, vol. 1, Dover, 1955.

Duncan, Robert. Preface. *Medieval Scenes*, Kent State University Libraries, 1978.

---. "Projective Project: Charles Olson." *Sulfur*, vol. 36, Spring 1995, pp. 25-43.

Falk, Jane. "Journal as Genre and Published Text: Beat Avant-Garde Writing Practices." *U of Toronto Quarterly*, vol. 73, no. 4, 2004, pp. 991-1002.

"Glyph." *Webster's Ninth New Collegiate Dictionary.* Merriam-Webster, 1983.

Guenther, Herbert V., translator. *The Life and Teaching of Naropa.* Oxford UP, 1963.

Johnson, Ronna C. "Three Generations of Beat Poetics." *The Cambridge Companion to American Poetry Since 1945*, edited by Jennifer Ashton. Cambridge UP, 2013, pp. 80-93.

Kolesnikoff, Nina. "Defamiliarization." *Encyclopedia of Contemporary Literary Theory*, edited by Irena R. Makaryk, U of Toronto P, 1993, pp. 528-29.

Kyger, Joanne. *About Now: Collected Poems.* National Poetry Foundation, 2007.

---. "Artist Statement." *Foundation for Contemporary Arts.* Foundation for Contemporary Arts, 2006, foundationforcontemporaryarts.org. Accessed 16 July 2019.

---. *Desecheo Notebook.* Arif Press, 1971.

---. Interview by Robert Bertholf. "Three Versions of the Poetic Line." *Credences 4*, vol. 2, no. 1, 1977, pp. 55-66.
---. Interview by Tyler Doherty and Tom Morgan. *There You Are*, edited by Cedar Sigo, Wave Books, 2017, pp. 134-37.
---. Interview by Lew Ellingham. "Taped interview, Lew Ellingham with Ebbe Borregaard and Joanne Kyger." 28 May 1982. TS. Courtesy the Estate of Joanne Kyger and The Poetry Collection of the University Libraries, University at Buffalo, The State University of New York.
---. Interview by Nancy M. Grace. "Places to Go: Joanne Kyger." *Breaking the Rule of Cool*, edited by Nancy M. Grace and Ronna C. Johnson, UP of Mississippi, 2004, pp. 133-53.
---. Interview by David Meltzer. "Joanne Kyger." *San Francisco Beat: Talking With the Poets*, edited by David Meltzer, City Lights Books, 2001, pp. 122-32.
---. Interview by Diana Middleton-McQuaid and John Thorpe. "Congratulatory Poetics." *Convivio*, 1983, pp. 109-20.
---. Interview by Chris McCreary. *Rain Taxi*. *There You Are*, edited by Cedar Sigo, Wave Books, 2017, pp. 139-42.
---. Interview by Lawrence Nahem. "A Conversation with Joanne Kyger." *Occident*, vol. 8, 1974, pp. 142-57.
---. Interview by Linda Russo. "Particularizing people's lives." *Jacket* 11, 2000, jacketmagazine.com/11/kyger-iv-by-russo.html. Accessed 14 Jan. 2020.
---. Interview by Dale Smith. "Energy on the Page." *Jacket* 11, 2000, jacketmagazine.com/11/ kyger-iv-dale-smith.html. Accessed 16 July 2019.
---. Interview by Anne Waldman. "Lokpala: Interview." *Civil Disobediences*, edited by Anne Waldman and Lisa Birman, Coffee House Press, 2004, pp. 289-93.
---. "Jane Falk Questions." Letter to the author. August 2010. TS.
---. *Joanne*. Angel Hair, 1970.
---. "Joanne Kyger." *Contemporary Authors Autobiography Series*, vol. 16, edited by Joyce Nakamura, Gale Research, 1992, pp. 187-203.
---. Letter to George Quasha. 18 Feb. 1969. TS. Courtesy the Estate of Joanne Kyger and Joanne Kyger Correspondence. MSS 8. Special Collections and Archives, UC San Diego Library.
---. *Lo & Behold*. Voices From the American Land, 2009.
---. *On Time*. City Lights Books, 2015.
---. *Places To Go*. Black Sparrow Press, 1970.
---. Personal Interview with the author. 15 July 2002.
---. *Strange Big Moon: The Japan and India Journals, 1960-1964*. North Atlantic Books, 2000.
---. *The Wonderful Focus of You*. Z Press, 1980.
Kyger, Joanne and Larry Fagin. "Letter from Paris." *There You Are*, edited by Cedar Sigo, Wave Books, 2017, pp. 44-46.

Norman, Charles. *Ezra Pound.* MacMillan, 1960.
Olson, Charles. *Mayan Letters*, edited by Robert Creeley, Jonathan Cape, 1953.
---. "Projective Verse." *Selected Writings of Charles Olson,* edited by Robert Creeley, New Directions, 1966, pp. 15-26.
Persky, Stan. Untitled with first line "the thing that is beautiful in me &." TS Courtesy the Author and Joanne Kyger Correspondence. MSS 8. Special Collections and Archives, UC San Diego Library.
---. Message to author. 28 Jan. 2018. E-mail.
"Poetics, Conceptions of." *Princeton Encyclopedia of Poetry and Poetics*, edited by Alex Preminger, Princeton UP, 1974.
Quasha, George. Message to author. 15 July 2019. E-mail.
Russo, Linda. "How You Want to Be Styled." *Among Friends*, edited by Anne Dewey and Libbie Rifkin. U of Iowa P, 2013, pp. 21-42.
Sanders. Ed. *Investigative Poetry*. City Lights Books, 1976.
Spicer, Jack. *The House That Jack Built,* edited by Peter Gizzi, Wesleyan UP, 1998.
Suzuki, D.T. "Aspects of Japanese Culture." *Evergreen Review,* vol. 2, no .6, 1958, pp. 40-56.
---. *Essays in Zen Buddhism*, 3rd Series. 1953, Samuel Weiser, 1970.
---. *Essays in Zen Buddhism*, 1st Series. Grove Press, 1961.
Waldman, Anne, and Andrew Schelling. Introduction. *Disembodied Poetics: Annals of the Jack Kerouac School*, edited by Anne Waldman and Andrew Schelling, U of New Mexico P, 1994, pp. xi-xiii.
Watten, Barrett. Introduction II. *A Guide to Poetics Journal: Writing in the Expanded Field, 1982–1998*, edited by Lyn Hejinian and Barrett Watten. Wesleyan UP, 2013, pp. 11-33.
Whalen, Philip. Untitled statement. *The New American Poetry*, edited by Donald Allen, Grove Press, 1960, p. 420.
Whalen-Bridge, John. "Poetry and Practice at Naropa University." *Writing as Enlightenment*, edited by John Whalen-Bridge and Gary Storhoff, SUNY Press, 2011, pp. 157-84.

Ted Talk
Aldon Lynn Nielsen

...hip carefully chooses its masks to confuse the pursuer, only to shed them with unexpected generosity at moments when he is least prepared for it.

— Marion Magid

The hipsters, alarmed at the simple life that all kinds of "niks" have crawled into, allowed modern junk sculpture to be thrown at the seedy bar where planted cedar trees often turned into street cars at half past on Sunday morns.

— Ted Joans

In 1973, the pop airwaves carried a question across the country posed by Oakland's invincible Tower of Power, "What Is Hip?" The song seemingly suggested that like the Tao, the truth was not to be, could not be, told:

> If you was really hip
> The passing years would show
> You into a hip trip
> Maybe hipper than hip
> But what is hip?

That suggestion also pointed prophetically to the conundrum faced by all hipsters of the present. The worst thing that can possibly befall a hipster is to be seen as being a hipster, which problem ill fits the obligatory uniform of stingy brim, skinny jeans, and lumberjack beard. Which makes the strange career of hip, now easing past a seventh decade, all the stranger.

Ted Joans was no stranger to hip. He often cast himself as a guide for the unhip, offering the services of his Rent-A-Beatnik company, writing handbooks, lecturing on the Beats. He even published a sort of guidebook to the hipster realm, titling it *The Hipsters*, though the backwards printing of that title on the rear cover was either a sly dig at the very idea, or something too hip for words.

The very idea; just a few short years later, people were beginning to wonder what had ever become of the hip. In June 1965, *Esquire* magazine's cover feature on James Bond was seemingly as hip as things got mid-sixties, but like the magazine itself, that was the hip of the Rat Pack, of the Mad Men, certainly not the Beat hip, which might rent itself for a Scarsdale party but certainly wasn't going to be found at the baccarat tables, and clearly preferred cannabis to cocktails, shaken or stirred. I know of that issue because in 1965 I was a fourteen-year-old boy with his own subscription to *Esquire*. My mother was not entirely approving of that subscription, probably because she recalled the racier *Esquire* of her own youth, a pre-*Playboy* place for titillation, and decidedly unhip. By the time I was reading the magazine, though, it had acquired a reputation as the publisher of some of the best fiction of the day and was pioneering what would soon be known as the New Journalism. While continuing a questionable gender politics, leaving the nakeder territories of the emerging sexual revolution to *Playboy*, *Esquire* had become increasingly discursive, but without ever losing its sense of humor. Sonny Liston appeared as Santa Claus on one cover, a fact apparently missed by Megyn "Santa Claus is white" Kelly. There were the magazine's annual Dubious Achievement Awards, and stunts like sending fiction writer Gina Berriault to cover the story of Carol Doda, San Francisco pioneer of silicone breast implants.

In that 1965 issue, there was a combination travelogue and think piece by Marion Magid, probably best known now as a long time editor of *Commentary* magazine. Magid's piece was titled "The Death of Hip." By now we are so used to writers declaring the invention of one thing and the death of another that we are not at all surprised to find that the article is less mordant than the title would imply, more in the nature of a search for whatever it was that was going to emerge from the ashes of Beat's hipsterdom. The piece opens with the expected epigraph from Norman Mailer's "The White Negro." Mailer's ruminations on hipness and race had already been subjected to a take-down collage by Ted Joans four years earlier, where the caption reads: "A white Negro is insolently received by some square maumaus who misunderstood his treatise on hipster theory" (n.p.). Magid sets out as a naif in hipland, but right at the outset she recognizes that what she is looking at is more singed phoenix than dead duck. "Something new and strange is in the air" (89), she writes, starting out from the East Village. She gets good advice from a transitional Beat there in the village. Much as Deep Throat just seven years later would advise Woodward and Bernstein to "follow the money" (this phrase is from the film, not from the book *All the President's Men*.) Magid's native informant, identifiable by her black leotards, tells her: "I don't know exactly what you're looking for, but follow the pot, and you'll find it" (89). Thus begins Magid's transoceanic search for hip, which takes her to London, Paris, Amsterdam, Berlin, Copenhagen, and finally back to the Village. Along the way, she talks with many of the hippest of the international Beats, including Alexander Trocchi and Jan Cremer. While Magid doesn't exactly ask her interviewees the questions Tower of Power were to pose to us, "What is hip? Do you think you know?" she is intent on tracing the ways that "the scene" found along the New York, Paris, Tangier routes of old was morphing into something else, while still mapping not just pot routes, but the routes of the potted.

Joans had been there, and would continue traversing the trade routes of Beat for the rest of his life, and it appears that Magid, on her journey of hip exploration, just missed him. Joans was featured in the second edition of Jean-Jacques Lebel's Free Expression Festival, during which, on the 20th of May 1965, Joans presented a poem titled "The Nice Colored Man." Magid may not have reached the North Africa of Bowles and Burroughs, but Joans did, and afterward reunited with Burroughs and Ginsberg in Paris. Joans would continue his itinerant life, while keeping a home in Mali for the remainder of his many days. His long, always in progress poem "Travelin'," which formally resembles Ginsburg's "Howl," is a picaresque assemblage. As it appeared in the collection *All of Ted Joans and No More* in 1961, it closed the book with a promise of opening. Joans tells his readers "TRAVELIN' will never be complete / until I stop traveling" (n.p.). That said, the unfinished "Travelin'," having trailed out at the end of *All of Ted Joans and No More*, appears not to have reappeared in Joans's subsequent collections, not even his late-life *Selected*, though the traveling itself remained central to his poetry and his poetics.

But if Magid didn't make it to Mali or Morocco, the European leg of her journey brought her meetings with wandering representatives of hip who had just come from or were just going to North Africa, carrying tales of Corso and Gysin along with their kit bags and stash. Were we to actually map the pilgrimage of Magid against the magical mystery tours of predecessor Beats, we'd see a tangled lineage leading to, well, what exactly? That was more or less the question she was asking at each stop on her journey. In city after city, she was found sitting in bars and squats, asking older Beats about the new hip, seemingly always looking in puzzlement at younger, yet longer-haired ambassadors of hip from the next generation. In London she reads *The Observer*, finding "a growing concern over why so much of English youth is now wearing its hair long" (90). *The Observer* helpfully published a full supplement on the question:

> Happenings: those antic spectacles, halfway between circus and psychodrama, designed to batter the spectator into new realms of awareness, are proliferating daily. What does it all mean? (90)

From my adolescent perch in Washington, D.C., I was observing much of what *The Observer* observed. The Corcoran Gallery of Art hosted a happening for our town, featuring Lloyd McNeill, a graduate of the famed Dunbar High School, Morehouse and Howard universities, who had worked with Owen Dodson and had spent the 1963-1964 academic year as artist-in-residence at Dartmouth. Sixties Washington was yet hipper than when it had given birth to Duke Ellington and the Washingtonians, and at its first acknowledged Happening, McNeill led his jazz band while his own art hung on the walls, actors acted, dancers danced, and journalists puzzled among the hipper attendees. "You know something is happening, but you don't know what it is," Bob Dylan sang around that time.

None of this was particularly puzzling to those of us who were coming onto the stage as the Beats aged into greater renown, but Magid was having a hard time putting two and two together. In Paris she visits Simon Posthuma of the Pot Art Company, chats with Maurice Girodias, who opines that Paris is dead, and asks habitues of the Café de Seine, "What is a hipster?" (94). They look incredulous. "I never liked that word," she reports hearing from John Esam." "The P-S-T lying there next to one another always got on my nerves" (94). What Magid hears is again a bit of broken Taoism: "Those who are, do not like to talk about it; but eventually they do" (95). But the trail eventually leads past Genet and others to resident West Indians, Lindsay Barrett and Dixie Nimmo, and that's when the Africa-West Indies-Hipster connection starts to manifest itself at last. We didn't need Mailer's screed to know that whatever hip was, it had always had Black inflections and African, or at least Africanesque, origins. The ocean currents of Modernity had swirled through Middle Passage and Triangle Trade, setting up the intellectual trade routes that led to an after-modern, and to hip. It falls to West Indian writer Dixie Nimmo, whose time in Paris encompassed friendships ranging from Chester Himes to Brion Gysin, to point Magid in the direction of Berlin and Ollie Harrington. Harrington, Nimmo promises, can be found by asking around among the musicians. He, we are assured, is "the last hipster of them all" (95).

Magid had been told first to follow the pot, then to ask the musicians. Her search finally turns up this possibly last hipster in East Berlin. One of her native informants had declared Berlin too cold for hipsters (98), but he had been driving a Mercedes, so who knows how hip he was to the hip geography of divided Germany. Once Magid finally tracks down Harrington, she poses the question directly: "What ever happened to hip, Ollie?" He responds:

> Once upon a time there was a small café called the Tournon, just a little old French café, that became the headquarters of a group of people...Dick Wright was one of them and Chester Himes was another and there was a third one, a painter named Beauford Delaney, and there was a fourth, a Nigerian called Slim Sunday, who dressed only in black leather and whose pet hates were Englishmen and tourists of any kind. (101)

What Harrington here describes is the African diaspora of expatriate artists who had gathered in Paris and had been in many ways the unacknowledged legislators of hip. What happened? According to Harrington's account, it was the same story of gentrification throughout history and across the globe. Art Buchwald, yes, Art Buchwald, wrote a column about the place "and before very long the tourists would come and just sit around and stare at the real live hipsters" (102), a perennial problem already lampooned by Joans in *The Hipsters*. Harrington goes on to trace the dispersal of these already dispersed hip artists, and describes his own migratory life that brought him in the end to be an East Berlin artist.

Harrington, like George Herriman of Krazy Kat fame, had been a forerunner of the underground comics that were bursting onto the scene even as Magid was filing her feature for *Esquire*. But where even an e.e. cummings would sing of Krazy Kat, Harrington's work was known to an overlapping audience that has always been there but seldom much analyzed by American culture watchers. Harrington was the creator of the *Bootsie* comic that ran in the *Pittsburgh Courier*. Magid reports that *Bootsie* was "another one of those things that every American Negro knows about and very few white Americans do" (100). We see from Magid's own accounts that she had not been among those very few whites before Dixie Nimmo had set her on Harrington's track. The very few whites who read Bootsie alongside "every American Negro" were the hipsters, who didn't much mind sometimes being the target of Bootsie's humor themselves. The October 17, 1959, issue of the *Courier* carried a Harrington cartoon in which Bootsie visits the studio of a very hip painter, who looks suspiciously like Ted Joans. "No, it don't make no sense to me neither Bootsie," the artist explains to his visitor. "But white folks 'jus wont buy nothin' if it makes sense!" This tracks with some of the early gossip around Joans, who was sometimes said to have taken up poetry after he saw other Beats making money with coffee house readings, and was similarly charged on occasion with keeping one eye on potential self-promotion while painting. Such charges were no doubt fueled by Joans's life-long talent for self-promotion and his history of wisecracks about his own motives, but greater credence should be accorded what Kathryne Lindberg has described as a "double address to history and fantasy in Joans's writing and painting." It doesn't take much looking to locate that double address even in Harrington's satire of Beat art, and yet what Joans was doing so often slipped from the sight of our cultural historians, even though he had never slipped off to East Berlin, like Harrington, and continued as an active writer and painter right through Black Arts, Hippies, and whatever we choose to call the present moment.

 Eliot Weinberger, for example, couldn't seem to see Joans. In a short appreciation introducing a selection of the poetry of Will Alexander in the journal *Sulfur*, Weinberger claimed Alexander as Aimé Césaire's sole American progeny, in the process wiping out a lineage that stretches from Langston Hughes through to Alexander himself. Hughes and Mercer Cook had been among the first to translate Césaire for an American audience, and his surrealist aesthetics had been central to African American verse (and hipness more generally) ever since. Weinberger would have done well to audit one of those lectures Ted Joans delivered on the evolution of "hipster" (note the circular window onto the hip) and the "hippie" (here enclosed in a confining square). Joans proclaimed that jazz was his religion and surrealism his point of view, and in his lectures he chalked those elements up as the animating features of what Magid had been trying to locate, the paths from hip to hippie. And along the margins of his central point, Joans wrote out a skeleton list of the names of the hip poets. Starting with LeRoi Jones, followed by Bob Kaufman, who for a time was nearly as neglected as Joans, the chalk talk, the Ted talk, identifies Tom Postell, early Village colleague of Baraka and Joans, and Bobb Hamilton, whose name here is misspelled. Hamilton, like Joans himself, made the transition into the Black Arts era as editor of the poetry journal *Soulbook*. Like Joans, too, Hamilton has often been disappeared, in one case literally. His poem "Upon Encountering a

Lost Love" was accepted by *Negro Digest* for its September 1965 poetry portfolio, but even though his name appeared in the table of contents, his manuscript, as the editors explained in November, "could not be located at deadline" (48). The poem was published along with an editorial apology in that November number. Even as Magid was searching out one Black artist, *Negro Digest* had been losing another. Joans's lecture notes also list Bernice Smart and Gloria Tropp, Black women artists and poets who have also been mostly disappeared from subsequent histories, even though Tropp's work was readily available on records and she performed at open mics into the 1990s.

Jayne Cortez, one of the many poets left out of the account by Eliot Weinberger, wrote in her poem "Nigerian/American Relations" that "They want the oil but they don't want the people." We could read that old *Bootsie* cartoon by Ollie Harrington as suggesting they want the oil paintings but they don't want the people. It might be said of the hipsterdom of the nineties and aughts that they wanted the culture but they didn't want the people. Two short years after Magid searched for the remnants of hip, the Summer of Love demonstrated what she had just begun to see glimpses of in her travels, the not always comfortable shading from hip to hippie. Surrealism came along for the ride, and some of the jazz, though Rock was in the ascendance. Sad to say, as anybody who read the R. Crumb comics and others of its ilk will remember, the racism, exoticism, and primitivism that animated western culture through Modernism, into the Beat era and beyond, was still very much in evidence. Hip hippies called Black people spades. Black people called Black people spades too, but like today's debates over the "n-word," that was another matter. Ted Joans had always been political, as evidenced in poems like "Dead Serious," written, as a note to the poem informs us, "behind the cotton curtain" from the back seat of a Greyhound bus" (n,p,). And so with books like *Black Pow Wow* and *Afrodisia*, Joans's work was right at home in the Black Arts Movement. His eroticism and capacious imagination also made his surrealist modes right at home in the midst of psychedelia. That much was prophesied in the 1960 poem "Is Your Fuzz Against My Junk." But where in the next decade the "colored girls" chorus of Lou Reed's "Walk on the Wild Side" gave many—including the backup singers themselves—the willies, when Joans spoke of colored girls, he was addressing a psychedelic futurity:

> I asked the pink girl and the orange girl to rock
> > instead of rolling
> > of course they refused and all the colored girls giggled

And while Joans's sexual politics may never have entirely caught up to the later times, we may at last be catching up to him. In "It Is Time," Joans chanted it is time

> for Afroamerican aardvarks and plaid rhinoceroses
> who are refused admission to the pink pig pen

schools and paletail lunch counter stools, to
refuse to wreck their trade in white Cadillacs
on the U.S. Die-ways

Just one year before Magid's pilgrimage, Sonny Rollins released "Now's the Time." We're still catching up to that music. Just a few years earlier, Joans had written that it was the time "for the Museum of Modern Art to show my paintings/ and the Library of Congress to publish my poems." A half century later, neither has happened, though one can find Ted Joans in the Library of Congress, and he does appear in The American Museum of Beat Art, though that's just a web site and Joans appears only as a writer; he is not on the Museum's list of visual artists.

The life of Ted Joans spans the entire history of hip; he lived until 2003, long enough to see the move from hipster to hippie and then back again to hipster. It may be that the second time "hipster" has returned as farce, but Ted still stands by his chalkboard, ready to tell us what was hip.

Works Cited

Hamilton, Bobb. "Upon Encountering a Lost Love" and editorial apology. *Negro Digest*, vol. 15, no. 1, November 1965, pp. 48.

Joans, Ted. *All of Ted Joans and No More: Beat Generation Jazz Poems*. Excelsior Press, 1961.

---. *The Hipsters*. Corinth Books, 1961.

Magid, Marion. "The Death of Hip." *Esquire Magazine*, vol. 63, no. 6, 1965, pp. 89-103, 138.

Improvisation c. 1959: Beat Film
Katherine Kinney

In November 1959, Robert Frank and Albert Leslie's *Pull My Daisy* and John Cassavetes's *Shadows* premiered as "The Cinema of Improvisation" at Amos Vogel's Cinema 16 film society in New York, founding the archive of Beat film. These films made now famous—and often refuted—claims to improvisation as both method and effect. The same year in *The Evergreen Review*, Jack Kerouac published his "Belief and Technique For Modern Prose: A List of Essentials," a manifesto for improvisational, spontaneous writing his own practice has likewise been criticized for failing to meet. Improvisation has long been recognized as a cardinal aesthetic virtue of Beat culture, with jazz, especially bebop, performance defining aspirational possibilities for Beat writing. By the late 1950s, cinema offered an alternative model of improvisation, one identified with what Paul Arthur has called "routines of emancipation" found both in the "ritual experience" of moviegoing and the promise of a widely available "domesticated technology" of movie making (3, 2). Energized by the new mobility of lighter-weight and less expensive 16mm cameras, as well as faster film stocks that did not require elaborate lighting set-ups, a range of artists and cineastes tried their hand at making films. Critic and aspiring filmmaker Jonas Mekas pronounced a New American Cinema and extolled its Beat aesthetic and affinity. In "New York Letter: Toward a spontaneous cinema," published in the *Monthly Film Bulletin* in 1959, Mekas describes a new generation of independent filmmakers distinguished by "their use of actual locations and direct lighting; their disrespect for plots and written scripts; their use of improvisation" (119).

Mekas was key to a lively discussion about improvisation and Beat film that emerged in 1959. As Daniel Belgrad argues, "A will to explore and record the spontaneous creative act characterized the most significant developments in American art and literature after WWII," Beat writing prominent among them (1). Beat cinema was a latecomer to what Belgrad has called "the culture of spontaneity." It emerged at the end of the 1950s in the wake of the popularization of the Beat generation as a literary movement and a cultural style. For Mekas, as for others, a Beat aesthetic was closely tied to the aspirations of a new American cinema. *Pull My Daisy*, Mekas writes, is "the first truly 'beat' film" not simply for its cast of Beat writers but because it typified the "expression of the younger generation's unconscious rejection of the middle-class way, the business man's way; an outburst of spontaneity and improvisation as an unconscious opposition to the mechanization of life" (120). In this context, cinema holds an ironic power as independent filmmakers sought to remake an industrial art form produced for a mass audience. "The First Statement of the New American Cinema Group" (1961) declared cinema an "indivisibly personal expression" and opposed its censorship, calling for new forms of financing and distribution for small budget films. Improvisation figures the creative gestalt seeking to free the cinema within a highly mechanized world.

I want to return to the hopes and hubris of 1959 to reconsider the claims made for improvisation, claims too often simply debunked as fraudulent. I focus on four films which were widely understood as Beat and improvisational in their moment: *Pull My Daisy*, *Shadows*, *Guns of the Trees* (Jonas Mekas 1962), and *The Connection* (Shirley Clarke 1961). The dedication to improvisation shared by these filmmakers was both intellectual and practical. John Cassavetes would become a director famous for his improvisational collaboration with actors. In 1958, he was a young actor finding success in commercial film, but so frustrated by the experience that he made *Shadows* as an experiment to free actors from conventional shooting practices. Robert Frank trained as a photographer in Switzerland before immigrating to the United States in 1947, where he quickly found recognition in New York. He began experimenting with a movie camera during his travels around the U.S., supported by a Guggenheim fellowship, in which he took thousands of photographs from which he composed his most famous collection, *The Americans* (1959), which was published with an introduction by Jack Kerouac. Albert Leslie had made films while in college at NYU where he studied art. By the late fifties, he was well established as a painter and wanted to move into filmmaking (Stein). With his "Movie Journal" column in *The Village Voice* and *Film Culture* magazine, Jonas Mekas supported the growing independent film community in the late 1950s. Mekas and his brother Adolfas immigrated from Lithuania as displaced persons in the wake of World War II. *Guns of the Trees* was his first film and, like his magazine, it was self-produced, made with the most minimal of financial support. Shirley Clarke began making films in 1954, earning acclaim for both her dance films and experimental shorts. In the late 1950s she worked for documentarian Willard Van Dyke. Their 1959 collaboration *Skyscraper* was nominated for the Academy Award for Best Short Action Live Film. *The Connection* was her first feature film, but she was by far the most experienced of this group of filmmakers.

Pull My Daisy, *Shadows*, *Guns of the Trees*, and *The Connection* offer various modes of improvisation, including creating characters through acting workshops, the use of non-professional actors, filming in uncontrolled locations, and a focus on unrehearsed quotidian activities. These techniques bring to life the Beat milieu of New York in the late 1950s and early 1960s. Mekas celebrates the "creative joy of the independent film artist, roaming the streets of New York, free, with his 16 mm. camera, on the Bowery, in Harlem, in Times Square, and in the Lower East Side apartments—the new American film poet, not giving a damn about Hollywood, art, critics, or anybody" (*Movie* 30). This "new American film poet" traverses the same New York neighborhoods invoked in Allen Ginsberg's "Howl." Many of the characters in these films, female as well as male, are artists (or artists manqué) living in ironic relation to the world of business. The films offer various forms of familial intimacy and communal association, moving beyond the tension between the heterosexual family and male sociality that animates *Pull My Daisy*.

Myths of pure improvisation surround *Pull My Daisy* and *Shadows* in particular. Critics, including Mekas, (mis)understood improvisation as an absolute value and have long obsessed over which moments in these films can be documented as unscripted, spontaneous actions captured by the camera. Such "capturing" is the subject of *The Connection*, in which a naïve director tries to force unrehearsed dramatic action into being. These filmmakers were all interested in the deeper transformative power of cameras, soundtracks, and editing. More than a recording of Beat life, Beat cinema elaborated new forms of improvisation, inscribing spontaneity into the very forms of mechanical reproduction that seemed to threaten it. In these films, the creative act of improvisation persists rather than dissolves in the face of writerly practices such as scripting and revision and the mediating technologies of filmmaking and moviegoing. Understood in this way, improvisation is not something that happens before the camera, but a variety of possibilities that happen in relationship to the camera.

As philosopher Gary Peters argues, improvisation has two distinct modes: a discourse of emancipation keyed to faith in self-expression and a pragmatic approach that makes use of the resources at hand. Beat cinema exemplifies a technical practice that embraces what Peters calls "the makeshift, the cobbled together, the temporary solutions to problems that remain unsolved," even as it aspires to a liberatory self-expression (9). *Pull My Daisy*, *Shadows*, and *Guns of the Trees* are representative of a committed "do-it-yourself" approach to filmmaking that rejected the high polish and narrative closure of commercial cinema. Presenting an often rough, imperfect surface and loosely plotted narrative structure, these films produced the effect of unscripted improvisation by abandoning naturalized commercial standards of narrative coherence and stylistic consistency. Mekas, for example, praises the technical weakness of *Shadows* as key to its break "with the official staged cinema, with made-up faces, with written scripts, with plot continuities. Even its inexperience in editing, sound, and camera work become part of its style, the roughness that only life [has].... The tones and rhythms of a new America are caught in *Shadows* for the very first time" (*Movie* 17). If Mekas's heady claims are echoed in accounts of a variety of underground filmmaking contexts then and now, the most radical potential of this moment of improvisational filmmaking can be seen in the opportunities afforded Black actors in *Shadows*, *Guns of the Trees*, and *The Connection*.

Jack Kerouac's narration for *Pull My Daisy* inspired some of the most absolute claims for improvisation. In his excellent history of the film's production, Blaine Allan catalogs contemporary descriptions of Kerouac's narration as "'spontaneous, unrehearsed,' 'off-the-cuff,' 'ad-libbed,' or 'improvised.'" He quotes Mekas's (approving) account: "without any preparation" Kerouac "just went on, as the images went by, in a sort of drunken trance; and his commentary has the immediacy and magic of such an improvisation" (Allan 185). Kerouac's published manifestos on spontaneous prose raised such expectations and helped defined the aspirational vocabulary used to describe cinematic improvisations: "Composing wild, undisciplined, pure, coming in from under, crazier the better" ("Belief" 57). Such claims supported criticisms as well as celebrations of the films, as Mekas himself acknowledged. In 1961, he began a column "On Improvisation and Spontaneity" with a parodic reference to the opening of Ginsberg's "Howl": "Whenever I mention *Shadows* or *Pull My Daisy*, I can hear groans from the best minds of the last generation." He quotes experimental filmmaker Maya Deren: "This spontaneous creation 'reminds me of nothing so much as an amateur burglar in a strange apartment…making one ungodly, clumsy mess'" (*Movie* 33). Deren condemns the often idealized practice of improvisation as artless and amateurish, rather than organic and inspired.

Kerouac's narration for *Pull My Daisy* complicates received notions of script, role, performance, and recording, engendering creative and critical possibilities denied when improvisation is understood as "ad-libbed" or "unscripted." The film's scenario was based on the third act of a play, *Beat Generation*, that Kerouac had written before Robert Frank approached him about collaborating on a film. As was his practice, Kerouac had recorded himself reading the play, voicing all the characters. That recording convinced Frank and Albert Leslie to have Kerouac narrate the film, voicing the various parts as he had on the tape recording. This allowed the film to be shot without sound, liberating the filmmakers from bulky sound equipment and the actors from microphones.[1] Kerouac recorded three complete takes of the voiceover in a studio, reworking his own material as he watched the film. The narration was then edited, drawing from the various takes, and synced to the film's images and actions. Editing has long been imagined as a technological mediation of performance antithetical to the spontaneity of improvisation, and one to which Kerouac reportedly objected. Allan argues that "Kerouac approached sound recording for its properties as an immediate record, not a constructive medium," and views Kerouac's resistance to the reconstruction of his recorded voice as analogous to his aversion to literary editors' revisions of his "spontaneous prose" (199).

According to Nancy M. Grace, however, Kerouac's spontaneous improvisations in poetry were "predicated upon, and often hid, his knowledge of oral and literary forms—vast structures undergirding what can appear disconnected, uncanny assemblages" (167). So too, as Grace documents, Kerouac's "verbal rehearsal" of stories, "was also complemented by revision and editing of large as well as small portions of spontaneously drafted texts. This latter practice, a secret reality undergirding his published manifestos, fueled his innovation predicated upon improvisation and spontaneity…" (33). *Pull My Daisy* originated in a dynamic exchange between spontaneous writing, voice recording, and revision that began before Frank and Kerouac ever discussed making a film. Rather than "capturing" a spontaneous outburst of poetry, the film's layering of sound and image extends Kerouac's improvisational work with words, images, and sounds. These layers are most evident when Kerouac narrates the music of Mezz McGillicuddy (David Amram) playing the French horn: "Jamambi, jamambi, jamac, jamac. And elder twine old tweezies fighted the prize. Jamambi, jamabi, jamambi, jamac." The written and performative qualities of improvisation merge as sense is subordinated to rhythm and sound, the beat and timbre of Kerouac's voice. In the finished film, his voice is accompanied on the soundtrack by Amram's music, music composed and recorded after the film was shot, layering different moments of improvisation in body, voice, performance, and composition.

Word play, a form of improvisation deeply associated with the Beats, runs throughout *Pull My Daisy*, binding Kerouac's narration to the characters and the rhythm on screen. Greg (Gregory Corso) asks the visiting Bishop, "Is it true that all the ignus that come falling inside the magic beer bottles magian candle stick?" and then explains apologetically, "I was goofing there...playing around with words."[2] There are numerous examples of such play in the narration: the list of subjects young Pablo (Pablo Frank) needs to learn at school: "geography and astromomology and pipliology and all them ologies, and poetologies, and goodbyeology" or the recitation of fourteen kinds of cockroaches ("melted cheese cockroaches, flour cockroaches, Chaplin cockroaches...") that ends the 360-degree circular shot at the dinner table. Even if written and rewritten, Kerouac's playful poetic catalogs are recognizable as improvisations, created through an intuitive, associative logic based on sound, repetition, and contiguity occasioned, for example, by Pablo leaving for school or the camera lingering on the (clean) kitchen. They are of the moment, but play past literal intersections of time and place, transforming the possibilities for the next line, image, action, or idea.

The antic playfulness of Kerouac's words and Ginsberg, Gregory Corso, and Peter Orlovsky's bodies in *Pull My Daisy* exemplifies the giddy fascination with sound recording and cameras central to Beat experience. The loose posture and anarchic posing of the poets embodies spontaneity, in vivid contrast to the propriety of the Bishop's visit. Ginsberg and Corso sit or lie on the floor, pouring over notebooks, until Ginsberg leaps about in a half squat, gesturing wildly. After Orlovsky arrives, the three poets crowd together on the couch, Orlovsky's arm affectionately draped about Ginsberg's head. Corso sits at the feet of the visiting Bishop (Richard Bellamy, credited as Mooney Peebles) in a pose of curiosity and mockery. When Ginsberg sits between the Bishop's mother (Alice Neel) and sister (Sally Gross) on the couch, he smiles with a faux innocence that Blaine Allan understandably compares to Harpo Marx (188). The Bishop's sister pulls down the hem of her skirt in response. The film pays careful attention to the small disruptions the poets generate, which elicit the anger of Milo's wife (Delphine Seyrig, credited as Beltiane). Such gendered responses allow the men to band together in apparently spontaneous rebellion against social expectations embodied in the film by women. But Ginsberg's smile also plays quite obviously to the camera, reveling in the performative possibilities its presence creates.

The film is much more than a home movie recording the spontaneous practice of Kerouac, Ginsberg, et al. The decision to have Kerouac voice all the characters breaks with the naturalizing assumptions of "lip sync" and the central place of dialogue in narrative film after the coming of sound. The separation in time between the recording of the actions of the bodies and the sound of the voice testifies to possibilities for improvisation that extend beyond the moment in which the actor performs before the camera. In other words, the creation of cinematic time through editing extends rather than compromises the freedom of improvisation. Moments when sound and image, voice and body fall into perfect sync become strange in the film. At one point, the poets "play cowboys," an act of improvisation offered as spontaneous: "something we've never done before," and born of moviegoing. Kerouac's narration momentarily falls perfectly in sync with the actors' gestures and speech—"pow" says Kerouac, as Milo (Larry Rivers) points his finger at Corso's forehead, who responds indignantly, his lips in sync with the words, "What'd you do that for?" The voice is clearly not Corso's any more than "pow" sounds like a gun. However, when the familiar technical relation of voice to body is restored so that character and "plot" work in sync, the improvisational dynamic seems to freeze. The separation of voice and bodies, soundtrack and image in *Pull My Daisy* creates a dynamic tension between elements of filmmaking that, according to convention, had been tightly synchronized; by doing so, the film makes apparent why improvisation as a break from scriptedness would become both metaphor and technique for the transformation of the cinema.

Shadows infamously ends with the proclamation: "THE FILM YOU HAVE JUST SEEN WAS AN IMPROVISATION." Written in bold letters across the neon lights of a New York street at night, this proud assertion strikes what Gary Peters calls the "major key" of improvisation's emancipatory discourse: "engaged and committed, rarely if ever ironic" (21). This major key is shared by critical responses to the film. A myth of improvisation became attached to *Shadows* from its premier, born of Cassavetes's unequivocal claim and intensified by the film's production history. A 60-minute version of the film premiered in November 1958, earning a distribution deal that required reuniting the cast to shoot new scenes in early 1959. That footage formed about two-thirds of the 90-minute version shown at Cinema 16 in November 1959 and in circulation ever since (Carney, *Shadows* 42-54). For Jonas Mekas, the 60-minute initial version of *Shadows* marked a radical break "with the official staged cinema, with made-up faces, with written scripts, with plot continuities," which was "ridiculously betrayed" by the revised version, which he dismissed as "a bad commercial film" (*Movie* 17). The dream of a lost, more perfectly original and improvisational *Shadows* has been nurtured by many critics over the ensuing years. Ray Carney has most extensively researched the differences between the two versions and reportedly found the holy grail, a 16mm print of the original version. His conclusion? The bold claim that ends the film is "a pack of lies." Carney's explanation is emphatic: "notwithstanding the final title card, at least two-thirds of the film was *not* an improvisation, but was written by Cassavetes in collaboration with a professional Hollywood screen writer. Every one of the scenes the critics praised in his masterpiece of improvisation had been scripted" (*Shadows* 8). The tenor of Carney's response shares the righteous outrage of Mekas's accusation of "betrayal."

There is ample evidence that in interviews publicizing the film Cassavetes exaggerated the speed and spontaneity of the filming and the degree to which they relied on direct sound recording (Carney, *Cassavetes* 62). The emphatic voice of these critics' responses, however, suggests a deeper disillusionment, one rooted in their allegiance to an ideal of improvisation as spontaneous personal expression that would emancipate filmmaking from commercial and technological complicity. What goes begging is a definition of improvisation except as what it is not: "official staged cinema, with made-up faces, with written scripts, with plot continuities" (Mekas, *Movie* 17). Improvisation in 1959 did promise freedom from the practices of commercial cinema, but it was not an abstraction. Improvisation was cultivated in a variety of institutions, most importantly in the case of *Shadows*, the acting workshop, which flourished in the post-war era. Philosophies and approaches may have varied but improvisation was widely practiced in these workshops, not as an end in itself, but as an experimental mode to explore situations, texts, and characters and to deepen collaboration among actors. Cassavetes's claim that *Shadows* is an improvisation, while misinterpreted by those who believed it as well as those who doubted it, is profoundly if not absolutely true.

Shadows was developed at the acting workshop founded by Cassavetes with Burt Lane in the mid-1950s. Cassavetes had a very specific motivation for making a film with the workshop; he wanted to liberate actors from their conventional relationship with the camera in commercial cinema. "I had worked [as an actor] in a lot of commercial films and I couldn't adjust to the medium," Cassavetes explained. "I found that I wasn't as free as I could be on the stage or in a live television show. So, for me, making *Shadows* was mainly to find out why I was not free" (Carney, *Cassavetes* 69). In commercial films, actors were constrained by myriad technical requirements: beholden to camera, sound boom, and lighting scheme, and monitored for continuity with regard to props, costume, focus, and other considerations from shot to shot. In the initial *Shadows* shoot, there was no screenplay and there were no rehearsals for the camera: no blocking established or marks to hit. The actors worked from character outlines and scenarios for a given scene—a familiar workshop format.

Cassavetes reversed the relationship of actor to camera: "We not only improvised in terms of the words, but we improvised in terms of motions. The cameraman also improvised. He had to follow the artists so that the actors could move when and wherever they pleased" (Carney, *Cassavetes* 72). The cameraman, Erich Kollmar, working with an Arriflex 16, "found that the lighting and photographing of these actors, who moved according to impulse instead of direction, prevented him from using a camera in a conventional way. He was forced to photograph the film with simplicity.... lighting a general area and hoping for the best" (Carney, *Cassavetes* 72). The original shoot of *Shadows* embraced amateurism and participation, with actors encouraged to take a turn operating the camera and a philosophy that refused to honor basic principles of continuity regarding focus and lighting.

The film's scenario originated as a workshop improvisation. Cassavetes told Hugh Hurd, Ben Carruthers, and Lelia Goldoni to play siblings. The actors initially protested that such a relationship would never be believed. Hurd was African American, Carruthers of mixed race, and Goldoni white. The dramatic catalyst for the scene turned on the shocked reaction of Lelia's white lover, Tony, when he meets Hugh and Hugh's angry response, a scene that remains important in the film. The initial improvisation went on for hours, engaging the actors and audience. Cassavetes felt he had found something that would work as the basis for a film. The characters and their relationships were defined through improvisations and developed in rehearsals at the workshop. The script for the second shoot was based on the performances previously created by the actors, a unique circumstance that reverses the assumption that actors are cast into pre-existing roles. Acting was thus the single most important element in the making of *Shadows*.

Many of the actors in the film were African American, for whom the possibilities of working without a script would have been especially liberating, given restrictive, racialized notions of character and casting. This possibility has never been given due consideration for two reasons: the persuasive narrative of a fresh and original improvisational film that was remade to conform to commercial conventions and the common description of *Shadows* as a racial passing film, a convention that has become less and less tenable over time. Scholars have focused on the drama of racial misidentification in the film, which echoes familiar tropes. So too, casting a white woman in the role of the Black woman who can pass was common practice in the studio-era. *Shadows*, however, does not conform to the principles of respectability, opportunity, and responsibility that shaped studio films such as *Pinky* (1949) or *Imitation of Life* (1959). Nor, is there any evidence Lelia is attempting to be accepted as white. David James offers the most sophisticated reading of this question, noting that "*Shadows* was vigorously innovative in paring down generic, histrionic, and photographic conventions….The maturity of its approach to racial and other social tensions is thus corroborated in the economy and immediacy of its style" (88). For James, however, "these same priorities and techniques also mark the social and aesthetic limitations of Cassavetes' project" (88). James understands the racial panic of Lelia's lover when he meets Hugh as the film's "structural center and thematic peripeteia" and finds Goldoni's casting a violation of credibility. He forcefully rejects the idea that any viewer could "accept that the plot should hinge on such a flimsy deception" (90). But is this moment as defining as James claims it to be? It seems a stretch of the imagination or an overdetermined acceptance of convention to see any action by Lelia's white lover, Tony, as the film's "structural center and thematic peripeteia."

I believe the intimacy between the three siblings forms the film's structural center and is a creation of the film's actor-centered, improvisational process of characterization. As Leila Goldoni recalled, in the original improvisation, "from the moment Ben playfully said, 'Hi sister!' the scene caught fire" (*bfi* 16). A scene from the second shoot exemplifies this intimacy, which has little to do with scripted features of dialogue or advancing a plot. Lelia lies in bed, ignoring Tony's phone calls on the morning after his poorly masked racial panic. The door to the bathroom is opposite Lelia's bed, and her brothers bicker good-naturedly about who gets first shower and where the towels are. Benny lies across the foot of Lelia's bed and tells her a "crazy" story about Charlie Parker. The camera emphasizes their proximity, shooting diagonally from the foot of the bed with Benny in the right foreground and Lelia propped on pillows to the left. The tight framing, like the close quarters of the apartment, captures a deep bond communicated through casual gestures of touch. Hugh tells Benny that Lelia is having a "little problem of the races," but that problem is not the story the scene tells. Rather, we see a family without parental authority or expectations, which nonetheless provides stability across the racial differentiation presumed to divide the characters. The focus on commonplace, undramatic actions and gestures in *Shadows* exemplifies the link between spontaneity and quotidian activity. The camera's attention to commonplace actions privileges affinity among characters over externally defined social roles. This, as much as the jazz soundtrack and nighttime wanderings of Benny and his pals, defines the film's Beat affinity.

The political struggle for desegregation necessitated the improvisation of new social relations and *Shadows*, like *Guns of the Trees* and *The Connection*, attempts, however imperfectly, to forego the familiar causality ascribed to race as character and plot in narrative films, but without ignoring racial difference. While the interracial family the actors create looks strangely contemporary today, Goldoni's casting raises the question of the access Black women had to the camera during this rich moment of experimentation. The apartment the siblings share is the center of a lively Black, artistic social world that includes white friends. A number of Black women have speaking parts in the film, but it is not clear whether any of them were members of the workshop. The workshop genesis gave lead roles in the experiment of making the movie to Hurd, Carruthers, and Rupert Crosse, as Hurd's manager, but, as far as I can determine, no Black actress shared fully in that opportunity.[3] In the four films under consideration in this essay, only one Black actress has a significant role: Argus Speare Julliard playing alongside Ben Carruthers in *Guns of the Trees*. Julliard and Carruthers were signatories to "The First Statement of the New American Cinema Group," as were Jonas Mekas, Robert Frank, Alfred Leslie, and Shirley Clarke. A short biographical note on the "Statement" says that Julliard appeared in *Shadows* as well as *Guns of the Trees*, but I have found no credit for her in the Cassavetes film or in any other subsequent production. Julliard has a powerful presence in *Guns*, but her career after is an archival blank. The actors featured in *Shadows* — Hugh Hurd, Lelia Goldoni, Rupert Crosse, and, to a lesser extent, Ben Carruthers — enjoyed successful varied acting careers.

More so than the other films, *Guns of the Trees* claims improvisation as a political as well as aesthetic principle. While filming, Mekas wrote in his diary, "What I want to achieve ideally with my film: is to overthrow the government. All governments. So we can start at the beginning" (Arthur 17). As Paul Arthur argues, Mekas "regularly employed political metaphors in framing the project of independent film," echoing the "general tendency to link the counterculture with resistance to capitalism [that] was augmented by a desultory identification with the struggles of Third World countries for self-determination" (17). Improvisation denotes an intentional artistic anarchy, or what Mekas called in notes for the film a "search for freer forms" ("While-U-Wait" 4). *Guns of the Trees* incorporates documentary footage from political protests against racial segregation, nuclear weapons, and U.S. policy in Cuba, as well from the 1961 Washington Square protest against the banning of folk music performers that came to be known as the "Beatnik Riot." The line between the fictional feature and such documentary moments is permeable, with the film's actors appearing within scenes of the protests as participants or passersby. Organized by chapters, the film eschews the connective causality of plot, moving back and forth in time without conventional markers to designate flashbacks. Mekas described the film's structure as "horizontal," lacking the hierarchal relationship among characters and action required for dramatic narrative. Such a horizontal structure remakes the relationship of the personal to the political. Like the freely mobile camera that takes notice of political action within everyday life, the soundtrack is liberated from the naturalism that binds it to an imaginary source within the image. An improvisational effect radically asserts itself in *Guns of the Trees*, insistently defying the conventions of continuity that traditionally make sense of cinema's layering of images, sound, and movement.

Mekas thus presses the quality of unscriptedness toward the limits of narrative coherence. The film relies on techniques that are intentionally disorienting for the audience. In a signed note at the opening of the film, Mekas declares, "The mad heart of the insane world has prevented me from finishing this film. It will remain rough, a sketchbook of what I intended it to be, an unfinished poem, a madhouse sutra, a cry." Echoing once again the language and images of "Howl," Mekas asserts the making of the film as an act of resistance. *Guns of the Trees* refuses to offer much in the way of exposition, relying on disjunctive shifts in time and place, as well as between soundtrack and image to create meaning. The film's strongest organizing structure lies in the contrast between two couples: one Black, Ben (Ben Carruthers) and Argus (Argus Speare Julliard), and the other white, Francis (Francis Stillman) and Gregory (Adolfas Mekas). Argus is pregnant and her relationship with Ben is marked by passion and play, despite the alienating office jobs that support their art (Argus is a painter, Ben a drummer). Francis, in contrast, has committed suicide before the film begins; she is often present, however, when the film makes abrupt shifts to the past.

Francis's suicide represents a broader existential despair. Pronounced through voice-over, the question "Why did Francis commit suicide?" hangs unanswered over the film. The voice posing the question is not identified with any character, offering a meta-level of narration that challenges realist conceptions of plot, character, and action. The questions of life and death that frame the film remain unanswered, symbolically signifying hope and despair rather than forming occasions for story. The film uses this and other sharp contrasts to generate meaning. For example, many scenes show characters walking along city streets only to cut without any narrative or visual transition to park-like settings or industrial wastelands. The apparent arbitrariness of location further disarms expectation so that actions the characters take may appear improvised, especially playful and joyous ones: a footrace down a corridor or clowning from the impromptu stage of a boxcar. On the other hand, a sequence of scenes that feature Gregory walking with a priest in Dominican-esque robes appears overdetermined symbolically, if not dramatically, and so lacks the same effect of spontaneity.

So too, the soundtrack often abruptly shifts between various forms of non-diegetic sound: voice-over, an air-raid siren, dogs barking, folksongs, harshly atonal music, and, most powerfully, Allen Ginsberg reading his poetry. The relationship of sound to image may appear makeshift, but often lacks a shared immediacy that would suggest an effective improvisation. Indeed, the harsh sounds of the dogs, air-raid siren, or atonal music can feel more like static, a violent intrusion on the image and the viewing experience even when a symbolic relation seems apparent. The relatively limited number of scenes with dialogue often feature formal poetic or philosophical turns of phrase spoken in ordinary settings such as offices or bars. These moments of dialogue rarely seem spontaneous or naturalistic, but neither do they offer exposition nor move the narrative forward. Scenes in which folksongs play or Ginsberg reads his poetry, however, share the rhythmic, associative immediacy similar to the improvisational effect in *Pull My Daisy*.

In a characteristic scene early in the film, we see Gregory walking New York streets followed by an abrupt cut to him standing in a field of tall, waving grass. An unidentified male voice asks, "Why does one commit suicide today?" The scene cuts back to the street and, as Gregory walks past people picketing Woolworth's Jim Crow segregationist policies (apparently unstaged), the voice is replaced by a non-diegetic air-raid siren, which perhaps answers the question regarding suicide. Under the siren's blare, Gregory playfully chases young girls skating on the sidewalk, an utterly unexpected sign of spontaneity and life, only to turn the corner where a dirty, ragged old man stands unsteadily. The siren fades and the film cuts to Gregory standing before a pile of scrap metal, machine engines blackened and forlorn, with a bare tree in the background revealed to sit at water's edge. After a few seconds of silence, we hear Ginsberg read the opening line of "Sunflower Sutra": "I walked on the banks of the tincan banana dock and sat down under the huge shade of a Southern Pacific locomotive to look at the sunset over the box house hills and cry," as the camera comes to rest on derelict engines.[4]

Ginsberg's poetry helps define the film's landscape, iconography, and emotional range, shifting expectations from the continuities of narrative progress to an associative logic and sensual expressiveness. At the most basic level, image and words are joined by the wandering both depict. Ginsberg's final words, "and cry," resonate with Gregory's restless state of mourning all the more strongly because we never see him cry. The high contrast black and white cinematography finds beauty in the wasted industrial landscape that accords with the imagery and sound of Ginsberg's voice, the consonance of *"tincan banana docks,"* for example. Here Mekas realizes the deep connection he imagined between a New American Cinema and a Beat aesthetic. So, too, Ginsberg gives voice to the connections the film draws between personal and political despair. In voice-over later in the film, Ginsberg indicts the American obsession with money and weapons: "I refuse to read the paper anymore!" he concludes in outrage. But he returns later in a sassy camp reconstruction of American history that begins: "What'd you say about my United Fruit? Don't be Nasty you lower class piece of trade. / I'll show you who's Miss Liberty or Not—."[5] The performative delivery of these lines feels improvised and demands an audience to appreciate the joke. The wistful, patient delivery of the line from "Sunflower Sutra" appears perhaps more immediately improvised, a personal expression that responds to the ruined landscape we see.

Balanced between elegy, outrage, and playfulness, Ginsberg's words enrich the lyricism of the film and reinforce the contrasting auras of despair and hope associated with the two couples. In the prologue to the film, Francis reads her apparent suicide note in voice-over, saying in part: "I've quit my job at the University and gone to buy honey doughnuts and come home to sit in the sunshine. I have four quarts of milk in the refrigerator. I wish the milkman would leave me alone. He will. So will they all." Her letter captures the way the film presents weighty and quotidian events with equal interest: protestors arrested by police at anti-nuclear demonstrations in Washington Square set against Argus cutting Ben's hair, for example. Francis finds no sustaining joy sitting in the sunshine; she clamors for meaning. Ben and Argus, in contrast, are depicted happily engaged in everyday activities: they make love, listen to the street through their open window, buy food and make coffee, dance and dream of the baby to come. They, too, struggle with the horror of the atomic bomb and the political climate: Argus is first seen sitting in her office, staring blank-faced at the camera as the air raid siren blares; Ben is outraged that Nixon is running for president. But the future calls them. The difference between the couples cannot be reduced to race. Yet, Ben and Argus's connection to the world around them, as well as their ability to imagine their child as a "new man," feels of a piece with the forward-looking moment of the Civil Rights movement. Improvisation becomes a political value in *Guns of the Trees*, revealing not only the terror of the moment, but the possibility of a better world.

The Connection offers a fitting ending point for this discussion as it turns a critical eye toward the romantic aspirations of improvisation and the "do-it-yourself" experimentalism of independent filmmaking represented by *Shadows*, *Pull My Daisy*, and *Guns of the Trees*. By bringing the camera into the frame, *The Connection* dramatizes the desire for improvisation and opens its aesthetic to debate. It too has a title card, signed by the fictional cameraman, J.J. Burden, who explains that the film's director left him with the footage they shot "in a drug addict's apartment early one evening last Fall. The responsibility of putting together this material is fully mine. I did it as honestly as I could." Unlike Cassavetes's boast or Mekas's cri de coeur, Clarke does not offer an authorial signature; this introduction remains within the diegesis of the film. The fictional Burden declares once again the makeshift, necessarily improvised nature of Beat filmmaking, but he lays claim to the professionalism of the documentarian rather than to the poet's purity of self-expression.

Tightly scripted and shot in 35mm with a union crew on a built set, the film was based on Jack Gelber's play of the same name, which was a surprise hit for the Living Theater in 1959. The play stirred controversy by offering the illusion of an actual group of addicts awaiting a fix as the producer and writer tried to cajole them into performance. The mixed-race cast, fascination with heroin use, dramatic scenes of shooting up and lancing a boil, and the permeable line between cast and audience exemplified the rejection of middle-brow artistic values central to the emergence of off-Broadway theater. Reviewers were deeply divided, but Gelber won the first Obie award for Best New Play and *The Connection* became a cause celebre in many artistic and intellectual circles. Improvisation is central to the play's aesthetic, which presents a production in process rather than completed. Cast interactions with the audience gave the stakes of improvisation a dramatic immediacy. This dramatic situation is unreproducible as an experience for the film audience. Clarke's film offers instead an interrogation of the limits of the documentary principles of direct cinema that were shaping the improvisational impulse of independent narrative fictional filmmaking in important ways. In the early sixties, the spontaneous possibilities enabled by lightweight, less intrusive cameras in documentary filmmaking gave rise to an idealized faith in the camera's objective ability to capture real life ("how things *really happen*," in the words of documentarian Richard Leacock), with "a minimum of interference or interpretation" (Rabinovitz 111). *The Connection* dramatizes the various ways in which the presence of cameras and filmmakers influences the people and events they observe.

In the film, a young white director, Jim Dunn (William Redfield), and experienced Black cameraman, J.J. Burden (Roscoe Lee Browne), are making a documentary about heroin addicts, a socially connected group of Black and white men who await their fix and then shoot up once their "connection" arrives. Set in a downtown flat, the film questions the distance between camera and event, as well as the artistic fascination with sub-cultures at the bottom of social and class hierarchies. The film presents the darker side of the Beat imagination, in which heroin offers a nihilistic revolt against conformity and confers a sometimes eloquent freedom of thought. As David Sterritt argues, the film "accompanies the existential liminality of the characters with a cinematic liminality of its own, reflexively exploring the margins between fiction and documentary style" (188-89). I argue that the film also questions the nature of improvisation at both levels, in the demands placed on the characters by the presence of the cameras and those placed on the filmmakers by their intense proximity to the everyday reality the characters both inhabit and represent.

"Just—act—naturally. The stuff you do every day is just fine," the director instructs his subjects in an increasingly strained desire to capture spontaneous real life. Working with two cameras, one stationary on a tripod and the other small and handheld, the fictional filmmakers demonstrate the elusive drama of everyday life within the relatively squalid presentation of drug addiction. As the film continues, Dunn finds it increasingly difficult to stay behind the camera, stepping into the frame in search of better camera angles, more interesting confessions, and visual interest. Dramatizing both direction and camerawork allows the audience to see the complicated dance between camera and subject required to film spontaneous action. The hectoring presence of the director and the quiet persistence of the cameraman animates Shirley Clarke's camera with a subjective, intentional address. Near the end of the film, the director attempts to film one of the addicts, Sam (Jim Anderson), telling a meandering story about evading the police. He yells at Sam that the story is "visually boring"; Sam picks up a hula hoop and tosses it with a back spin that returns it to him. The camera follows the hoop back and forth until Sam fakes the next toss. The camera moves where the hoop was expected to go but doesn't. "Ha!" Sam barks a sharp laugh, and points at the camera with a knowing smile. If quotidian activity is one of the marks of improvisational filmmaking, *The Connection* demonstrates the desire the camera signifies to elicit the dramatic within the ordinary.

Earlier in the film, Sam is told he has to "pay his dues" and tell his story for the camera, the price of the awaited fix paid for by the director. He turns a sharp appraising eye to the camera and asks, "What do you want, Jim Dunn?" before capitulating. "Alright, I can do the old soft shoe," he says to the camera, "I don't even need cork." This allusion to the blackface makeup of minstrelsy reframes the documentary camera's address within cinema's long history of racist exploitation of Black performance as entertainment.[6] A petty thief, Sam appears to be the film's least sophisticated character, but his canny improvisations reveal the economics of exchange that define his performance and frustrate the director's desire for a transparent access to reality. Increasingly, the director loses his place in the story. The professional proximity and objectivity promised by his modern handheld camera is compromised by the white privilege and affluence it also signifies. J.J.'s signature on the film's title card offers surprising testimony to the failed transparency of whiteness aligned with the camera.

One of the finest moments of performance comes late in the film, when Dunn's frustration overflows and he taunts Cowboy (Carl Lee), "I was going to make you the hero of this film." Up to this point, Cowboy has been an unflappable presence as the connection the other men depend upon. Dressed in impeccable white, he has a soothing voice and carries his tall thin body with a loose, easy patience. He sits filing his nails as Dunn pounds the table, but when told, "Go on, like say something," Cowboy stands, eyes locked on Dunn now off-camera, and leans over the table. "It's too much risk!" he explodes, punctuating each word and slapping his hand on the table. "To go out and score every night! I mean, man, I'm followed every night and have to scheme a way to get back here." His voice rising, he proclaims, "I'm tired. Man, I've been moving my whole life." He falters, seeming about to nod out, and then raises his eyes, "Now is that what you wanted, Jim?" he asks, slyly drawing out the director's name in a mocking, jive delivery. The spectacle of a command performance, the demand placed on the Black man to act as himself, allows Carl Lee as Cowboy to claim a double register of address that exceeds the character and comments on the film itself. That roles and lines are scripted is beside the point. There is too much risk entailed, not only by being the connection for this fragile community, but in the promise to be "made" the hero of the film by an increasingly demanding, obtuse, and hostile white director. The risk is also more basic: the possible cost for a Black man, whether character or actor, in revealing himself to the all-too-present camera. The moment of truth Dunn seeks comes at his own expense, in a surprising moment of performance that captures the duality of improvisation as an inspired response that exposes the demands of the moment.

The debates about the nature and value of improvisation in Beat film that emerged in 1959 remain richly generative today. The faith in spontaneity so central to Beat literature was elaborated in independent filmmaking in New York at the beginning of the 1960s. The assertion of improvisation, even in claims as unequivocal and unqualified as Cassavetes makes at the end of *Shadows*, should not be understood as either true or false. Rather, we need to ask how improvisation was practiced during production, how it manifests in a film, what changes it enabled in the paradigms of commercial cinema, and the variety of aesthetic, social, and political values it expressed. *Pull My Daisy*, *Shadows*, *Guns of the Trees*, and *The Connection* are Beat films less for their representation of Beat sub-culture, than because they were recognized as harbingers of change closely aligned with the bold literary art of Kerouac, Ginsberg, Corso, and others. Philosophically, Beat cinema formed an early chapter in what Paul Arthur calls the "utopian conviction" that found its "consummate expression" in American culture of the 1960s: that cinema offered "an emblem, harbinger, and social vehicle of the transfiguration of time, heralding a phenomenology of an eternal present made image" (1). This transfiguration does not "capture" the moment of the present; it creates it, giving it form and expression in the collective home of the movie theater. The promise of a "phenomenology of an eternal present" allows the highly produced and technologically recorded art of filmmaking to inscribe an idealized effect of improvisation.

Arthur's description of a cinematic phenomenology of time accords with Kerouac's claim in "Essentials of Spontaneous Prose" that "Nothing is muddy that *runs in time* and to the laws of time" (72). This context helps make sense of how and why movies loomed large in Beat imagination and aesthetics. Kerouac ends his "List of Essentials" for the "Belief and Technique of Modern Prose" with two references to the movies bracketing more apparently representative claims to romantic self-expression:

> 26. *Bookmovie is the movie in words, the visual American form*
> 27. In praise of Character in the Bleak inhuman Loneliness
> 28. Composing wild, undisciplined, pure, coming in from under, crazier the better
> 29. You're a Genius all the time
> 30. *Writer-Director of Earthly movies Sponsored & Angeled in Heaven*
>
> (57, my emphasis)

Movies offer a mirror of the imagination, one which accords with Kerouac's "belief" in technique in crucial ways: running in time, in images, words, music, and sound. Beat cinema was in Arthur's terms a "routine of emancipation" closely aligned with the freedom of expression claimed in "Howl," *On the Road*, and other works of Beat literature and engaged in parallel forms of improvisatory exploration.

Notes

1. Small cameras, such as the 35mm Arriflex used to film *Pull My Daisy*, had to be encased in heavy "blimps" to muffle the sound of the motor in order to record sound simultaneously. Sound recording equipment itself was awkward and heavy until the Nargra III sound recorder became available just after the period in which these films were made. Technical and budget limitations meant that independent filmmakers often had to choose between free movement and simultaneous sound recording.
2. When quoting Kerouac's narration, I rely on the transcript included with the Steidl DVD. No page numbers are included.
3. In the little seen film *An Affair of the Skin* (Ben Maddow 1963), Diana Sands plays a photographer living in Greenwich Village whose movements through the city are filmed with improvisational techniques akin to those of Beat cinema. Sands' performance is a rare example from the period that allows a Black woman the freedom of mobility so central to Beat film. See Kinney (84-86).
4. The film was recorded before publication of "Sunflower Sutra." In the film Ginsberg reads from a not yet finished draft.
5. This poem, "Subliminal," which to my knowledge was never previously published, can be found in the 1977 edition of Ginsberg's journals from the early sixties (156-57).
6. See Michael Rogin's account of the role played by minstrelsy in consolidating the Hollywood audience in films including *Birth of a Nation*, *The Jazz Singer*, and *Gone with the Wind*, as well as its legacy in the postwar period. Sam's knowing address to the camera can be placed within the alternative history documented by Miriam Petty in her groundbreaking research on Black performers and audiences in the 1930s.

Works Cited

Allan, Blaine. "The Making (and Unmaking) of 'Pull My Daisy.'" *Film History*, vol. 2, no. 3, 1988, pp. 185-205.
Arthur, Paul. *Line of Sight: American Avant-Garde Film Since 1965*. U of Minnesota P, 2005.
Belgrad, Daniel. *The Culture of Spontaneity: Improvisation and the Arts in Postwar America*. U of Chicago P, 1998.
Carney, Ray, editor. *Cassavetes on Cassavetes*. Farrar, Straus and Giroux, 2001.
---. Shadows *BFI Film Classics*. British Film Institute, 2001.
Cassavetes, John. *Shadows*. 1959. Criterion, 2008.
Clarke, Shirley. *The Connection*. 1961. Milestone Film and Video, 2015.
Frank, Robert and Alfred Leslie. *Pull My Daisy*. 1959. Written and Narrated by Jack Kerouac, Steidl, 2012.
Ginsberg, Allen. "Howl." *Howl and Other Poems*, City Lights Books, 1980.
---. *Journals: Early Fifties Early Sixties*, edited by Gordon Ball, Grove Press, 1977.
Grace, Nancy M. *Jack Kerouac and the Literary Imagination*. Palgrave Macmillan, 2007.
James, David. *Allegories of Cinema: American Film in the Sixties*, Princeton UP, 1989.
Kerouac, Jack. "Belief and Technique for Modern Prose." *Evergreen Review*, vol. 2, no. 8, 1959, p. 57.
---. "Essentials of Spontaneous Prose," *Evergreen Review*, vol. 2, no. 5, 1958, pp. 72-73.
Kinney, Katherine. "Facing the Camera: Black Actors and Direct Address in Independent Films of the 1960s." *Journal of Cinema and Media Studies*, vol. 59, no. 1, 2019, pp. 66-88.
Mekas, Jonas. "The First Statement of New American Cinema Group." 1961. *Film Culture Reader,* edited by P. Adams Sitney, Praeger, 1970, pp 79-83.
---. *Guns of the Trees*. 1962. Re:voir, 2012.
---. *Movie Journal: The Rise of New American Cinema, 1959-1971*. 2nd ed., Columbia UP, 2016.
---. "New York Letter: Towards a spontaneous cinema." *Monthly Film Bulletin*, vol. 28, no. 3/4, 1959, pp. 118-21.
---. "While-U-Wait." 1962. Booklet included with *Guns of the Trees*, DVD, Re:voir, 2012, pp. 4-5.
Peters, Gary. *The Philosophy of Improvisation*. U of Chicago P, 2009.
Petty, Miriam. *Stealing the Show: African American Performers and Audiences in the 1930s*. U of California P, 2016.
Rabinovitz, Lauren. *Points of Resistance: Women, Power and Politics in the New York Avant-garde Cinema, 1943-1971*. U of Illinois P, 1991.
Rogin, Michael. "'Democracy and Burnt Cork': The End of Blackface, the Beginning of Civil Rights." *Representations*, no. 46, 1994, pp. 1-34.

Stein, Judith. "Alfred Leslie: An Interview." *Art in America*, August 5, 2016.
Sterritt, David. *Mad to be Saved: The Beats, the '50s and Film*. Southern Illinois UP, 1998.

State-of-the-Field
Survey of Current Scholars

Introduction

After more than half a century, critical literature on the Beat generation has emerged as a dynamic subfield in American literary history, the subject of numerous journal articles, anthologies of literary criticism, biographies (22 alone of Jack Kerouac), memoirs, dissertations, interviews, and edited volumes of journals and correspondence. Early critics produced readings upon which scholars and course instructors still rely: *A Casebook on the Beat* (1961), edited by Thomas Parkinson, features criticism by Henry Miller and Warren Tallman; Mary McCarthy reviewed *Naked Lunch* for *Encounter* (1963); John Tytell composed *Naked Angels* (1976); and Tim Hunt brought out *Kerouac's Crooked Road* (1981). Beat literature has also received attention in significant scholarly journals, including *American Literature, Texas Studies in Language and Literature, College Composition, College Literature*, and *Contemporary Literature*. Exhibitions have been hosted by major art museums, notably the Whitney Museum of American Art's 1995 "Beat Culture and the New America, 1950-1965" exhibit. Academic associations—the Beat Studies Association (BSA) and the European Beat Studies Network (EBSN)—now exist; the Modern Language Association, the American Literature Association, the University of Louisville (Literature and Culture Since 1900), and the Popular Culture Association have all hosted multiple sessions devoted to Beat writers. Many social media sites now focus on Beat literature and culture, and Clemson UP/Liverpool UP has recently introduced the Beat Studies Book Series. Beat generation authors have also been awarded significant literary prizes, including international recognition with the 2016 Nobel Prize in Literature going to American poet-songwriter Bob Dylan, whose art descends in part from Kerouac and Ginsberg. And, of course, the monumental scholarship of Ann Charters, in many respects the founder of Beat Studies, cannot be ignored.

The 1980s and 1990s saw the emergence of recovery research, particularly on the women writers associated with the movement, a line of inquiry instigated by Joyce Johnson's powerful memoir *Minor Characters*. The intersecting concepts of race, gender, sexuality, and class have led to increased scholarship focused on Beat representations of women and people of color. Work on Beat film, music, drama, and spirituality has also deepened the field, as has a focus on the transnational and international aspects of Beat writing and criticism. Much of this wide-ranging research draws upon traditional archival study and utilizes challenging contemporary theoretical methods of investigation.

While relatively new lines of research have succeeded in strengthening understanding of the complex realities of Beat lives and literature, challenging Beat hagiography while extolling Beat practices that have contributed to 21st-century art world wide, we ask where the future of Beat Studies lies. The question is essential for the continued viability of Beat literary art as well as its academic partner—criticism of Beat literature. For this reason, in the spirit of investigative criticism, we have posed two broad questions to members of the Beat Studies Association and a few other scholars:

1. What do you believe to be the current state of the field of Beat Studies and why? Answers can address the field locally, nationally, or internationally; in terms of literary innovations, literary theory, politics, intersections with other fields, science and technology; etc. We're interested in your ideas without constraints.

2. What topics, literary approaches, critical perspectives, etc., do you believe should be the focus of Beat Studies as it moves forward and why? In other words, what types of articles, features, etc., would you like to read in journals such as ours?

With both, we encouraged honesty and fresh thinking in statements ranging approximately from 250 to 500 words. We thank the 28 respondents, presented below in alphabetical order, for taking the opportunity to assess the field, a move that we hope creates an on-going conversation of the kind sometimes overlooked in the humanities. Such conversations, many of which only take place in brief email exchanges or amongst a handful of conference presenters, drive the intellectual life of our professional work.

Readers will find in the following statements several recurring themes, particularly recognition of the growing maturity of the field, upholding the high standards of early critics such as those noted above, through research on previously unstudied women Beat writers, Beat writers of color, and the transnational focus on Beat culture's impact. Some respondents call for more work in these areas, while others turn toward interdisciplinarity, media and digital studies, environmental studies, public policy, and a more honest recognition of the problematic histories of some Beat writers. Several note the lingering misperception in higher education regarding the legitimacy of Beat literary methods and poetic practices. Many other remarks complete a collection that in total projects faith in the field along with energy, creativity, and intellectual passion for our work.

STATE-OF-THE-FIELD SURVEY

The Responses

STEVEN BELLETTO
Professor of English, Lafayette College, Easton, Pennsylvania

I continue to be amazed by the energy and range of critical work produced under the banner of Beat Studies. Beat Studies has matured significantly over the past several decades, especially as students and scholars now have an impressive array of institutional supports—not only the *Journal of Beat Studies*, but the new Clemson UP/Liverpool UP Beat Studies Book Series as well as the BSA and EBSN. And every few months, it seems there is another book exploring individual authors or taking deeper dives into how we understand the Beats as a movement. This is all to the good. That said, in my experience, there remains within the academy lingering misperceptions about Beat-associated writers. To indulge a quick anecdote: I was speaking with a well-known scholar of early modern literature and critical theory, and he expressed surprise when I mentioned recent work bringing, say, Deleuze, to bear on, say, Kerouac, or work that takes seriously the political dimensions of Ginsberg's poetry. This scholar said something about how Beat writers had little regard for technique, and so Deleuze's philosophical curlicues would be wasted on such trivial subject matter. This was in 2019. I was a little surprised by this strangely confident pronouncement, even as it wasn't the first time I encountered it; for this reason, I would still be hesitant to advise doctoral students to write dissertations solely devoted to Beat writers because I think it would make an already seemingly-insurmountable job market even more challenging.

While writing *The Beats: A Literary History*, I discovered I was grateful for work that attended to the material history of Beat-associated writing: so often this writing appeared in hard-to-find places—or may remain unpublished—and so it was enormously useful for me when fellow scholars had taken the time to sort through archival material to produce stable editions from which to work. Not only do such volumes confer legitimacy on individual writers, but they provide starting points for those exploring the Beat movement from more capacious perspectives. To that end, I would be very happy to see work of this sort done in connection to wider arrays of figures (Ted Joans, Bob Kaufman, Kay Johnson, Tuli Kupferberg, Barbara Moraff, and Ray Bremser would have my early vote). In terms of the *Journal of Beat Studies*, I would be excited to see a feature on little-known Beat-associated writers and texts—something along the lines of *PMLA*'s "little-known documents" feature. It would be useful if a specialized venue like the *Journal of Beat Studies* had a regular feature introducing readers to thumbnail biographies of more obscure figures, or even to brief analyses of little-known texts that might merit further study. I'd certainly be interested in further scholarship on the Beats and political considerations, particularly with respect to the cold war rhetorical frame and questions of neocolonialism and postcolonialism; on the Beats and the anthropocene; and on what the Beat fascination with the self may tell us about our own contemporary social media moment.

ROBERT BENNETT
Professor of English, Montana State University, Bozeman, Montana

The state of Beat Studies has never been stronger. In particular, Beat Studies has finally established a solid foundation in the academy. Innovative new monographs, compelling literary histories, and comprehensive anthologies are now published on a regular basis, and academic conferences and journals now broadly cover Beat topics as full-fledged contributions to mainstream academic scholarship. Beat Studies is no longer considered merely a fringe or niche subject matter, let alone beneath the dignity of serious academic analysis. Equally importantly, the Beat canon has been expanded to include an extensive array of women, minority, and international Beat figures, providing a more comprehensive and more representative understanding of the larger Beat movement as a whole. Not only are more Beat writers now studied in more venues than ever before, but a bright future for Beat Studies now seems certain. The past generation of Beat scholarship has accomplished a truly monumental task: it has completely altered the viability of Beat Studies, finally providing it with a firm foundation which promises to make the increasing visibility, even prominence, of Beat authors all but irreversible. Beat Studies qua Beat Studies has truly come of age.

If there is one new direction that I would like to see in Beat Studies, however, it would be a fuller integration of Beat scholarship within literary and cultural studies more broadly conceived. As it is, too often Beat writers are studied as an island unto themselves: as exemplars of a viable, but distinct, almost isolated, Beat movement. Beat Writers are too infrequently analyzed in connection with other non-Beat writers as part of larger trends that include but also extend beyond Beat culture. The Beat movement has important things to say about the American West, the Pacific Rim, environmentalism, the borderlands, globalization, the history of madness, improvisation studies, oral poetics, interdisciplinary relationships between literature and music, and so many other topics, but all too often when these issues are addressed with respect to Beat culture there is little consideration of how these issues are also engaged, in similar yet distinct ways, by other writers representing different literary and cultural traditions. In short, while Beat Studies itself has flourished, I would like to see the Beat Generation talked about and analyzed more extensively outside of the narrow confines of Beat Studies. Now that Beat Studies has established itself as an academic subfield, that subfield itself needs to be better integrated into the broader currents of literary and cultural studies at large. This task will provide ample opportunities to engage a new generation of Beat scholars in new directions that can only further emphasize the larger cultural significance of Beat culture.

STATE-OF-THE-FIELD SURVEY

DAVID STEPHEN CALONNE
Lecturer, Eastern Michigan University, Ypsilanti, Michigan

It seems clear that Beat Studies has increased in visibility and significance the past decade, due in large part to the fact that American society has become more tolerant of many of the issues the Beats advocated: rights for those who identify as non-heterosexual, ecological awareness, and acceptance of the "non-white minorities" of our country. Also, several of the critical fields which have opened up following the rise of "deconstruction"—queer studies, cultural studies, the intersection between pop or "low" culture and "high culture," "virtual reality," etc.—have encouraged scholars to pursue intersections between authors such as Kerouac, Burroughs, di Prima, Corso and Ginsberg, for example—and contemporary critical theory. The recent appearance of a text such as *William S. Burroughs: Cutting up the Century* (2019) suggests that scholars are turning to what were once considered to be "avant-garde" or "daring" literary experiments as worthy of serious examination. It is also clear that prestigious publishers such as Cambridge University Press have become increasingly active in their pursuit of topics related to Beat literature and I think this is also a sign that what had before been considered to be a field outside the "mainstream" has now begun to enter the ivory towers....

There are several possibilities for ways of presenting essays in a literary journal such as the *Journal of Beat Studies*. One avenue of approach might be to take a single theme such as "The Occult/Magic/Esotericism" in the work of the Beats—a topic I have pursued the past several years—and invite papers on this topic. Or specific critical approaches such as gender, post-modernism, cultural studies, etc. could provide ways to focus a particular issue. Or intersections between the Beats and art, music. How did a figure like Charles Olson influence the Beat approach to Mexico or to the ancient world—a topic explored to some degree in the book *The Hip Sublime*?

MARY PANICCIA CARDEN
Professor of English, Edinboro University, Edinboro, Pennsylvania

The field of Beat Studies is at a particularly dynamic, expansive stage in its development, thanks to the ongoing efforts of committed and energetic organizations and individuals. The Beat Studies Association and the European Beat Studies Network play crucial roles in keeping the field vital and drawing in more scholars. The BSA continues to maintain a Beat Studies presence at important conferences in the U.S., and the EBSN deserves special commendation for its lively conferences. Of course, the *Journal of Beat*

Studies serves as an essential venue for rigorous and innovative scholarship and research on the Beats and associated writers and artists. Work being presented at conferences and published in *JBS* is strikingly various and diverse; it challenges conventional thinking about who Beats are, what Beat is, where Beat reaches, and what sorts of issues and questions Beat legitimately addresses.

I very much appreciate *JBS* interviews and articles that provide access to lesser-known figures and have been consistently impressed with and grateful for the depth and quality of the journal's book reviews. I am inspired by both the quality and the quantity of new scholarly books on the Beats and by the ongoing publication and republication of work by Beat-related writers. I think that in concert with *JBS*, the establishment of the Clemson UP/Liverpool UP Beat Studies Book Series marks an important turning point. I'm particularly excited about the potential for a book of essays on teaching the Beats; I believe its publication will spur new courses that will attract new generations of readers and likely bring more scholars into the field.

Since Beat Studies now has outlets for scholarly publication, I think it's time to work on other, associated ways of encouraging innovative research. I think we could support a U.S. conference (perhaps biannual) devoted to Beat Studies. I would love to see a searchable digital archive of primary sources, especially out of print texts and hard-to-find work from obscure, small, or short-lived independent publishers. I would also love to see a regular feature in the *Journal of Beat Studies* that reprints pieces from independent magazines and newsletters, especially work by lesser-known writers.

I think many of us would appreciate a way of sharing teaching experiences and strategies, maybe on the BSA website or the Beat Generation Studies "hang out" at the MLA Commons. Perhaps this topic could become the basis of a feature in *JBS* as well.

JEAN-CHRISTOPHE CLOUTIER
Associate Professor of English, University of Pennsylvania,
Philadelphia, Pennsylvania

My sense is that Beat Studies today is moving toward a more inclusive, internationalist approach, while also making forays into studies of new media and transmedia, including material text studies. Perhaps Beat Studies is at a crossroads—and has been for a while—between scholarship that used to rely heavily on biography and anecdotal sensationalism, and scholarship that concentrates on Beat textual and media innovations, on genetic analysis of manuscript drafts, on *longue durée* internationalist scope, on their placement within varied literary traditions, and on multilingualism/multiculturalism. Anthologies like *Reconstructing the Beats* or the more recent *Cambridge Companion to the Beats* contain examples of such exciting new directions for Beat Studies. As a Québécois,

I also feel obligated to note that "Beat Studies" is its own "thing" depending on the nation out of which one asks the question.

Beat Studies continues to face challenges to its legitimacy as a field. In an age when much of academic labor—and rightly so—is dedicated to dismantling patriarchal discourse and white supremacy in knowledge production, the original trio of Kerouac/Ginsberg/Burroughs inevitably continues to be out of favor in many intellectual circles. Beat Studies needs to deal, in as honest and direct a fashion as possible, with the often-problematic identity politics of many writers and artists associated with the Beat movement. If Beat Studies continues to ignore this messy reality, or fails to take it seriously, or sees it as a passing fad, then as teachers I fear we will continue to lose our audience, and Beat works will slowly fall into obscurity as yet another cluster of work from a racist and misogynistic band of privileged white folks.

I hope Beat scholarship can emphasize the craft, the labor and toil, and the years of dedication Beat authors gave to the rigorous study of a multiplicity of literary, philosophical, and religious traditions. I'd love to see more material text studies of Beat works, studies on the contemporary legacy of the Beats, studies that reckon with Beat identity politics framed not as easy disavowal or a call for "cancel culture" but rather as deep historicist engagements that help readers understand the original time of composition, the ideologies that helped form their positions, and that continue to inform our current moment. I'd love to see essays that compare the conformism of the postwar period in the U.S. to today's new forms of conformity and extreme political factioning. New assessments of peripheral Beat figures are also always welcome, especially when these help us recuperate minority voices.

At times, too much familiarity rises in some strands of Beat Studies, which undermines its authority. Many essays refer to Kerouac as "Jack" rather than his last name—this never happens in Nabokov studies, for instance (no one says, "As Vladimir says"), so a healthy dose of critical distance might help. The "telepathic shock and meaning excitement" is ours as fans, but as scholars I'd like to see us treat Beat authors with the gravitas they deserve through basic scholarly conventions.

LESLIE STEWART CURTIS
Professor of Art History, John Carroll University, Cleveland, Ohio

Since the Whitney's "Beat Culture and the New America, 1950-1965" exhibition (1996), the field of Beat Studies has increasingly expanded to include visual arts. The Pompidou Center's *Beat Generation* show (2016) included the full-length typescript of Kerouac's *On the Road*, Brion Gysin's *Dreamachine*, Kerouac's paintings and drawings, and photographs by Burroughs and Ginsberg. Unfortunately, only a few art works hinted at the much broader diversity of relevant artists, although a video showed Ginsberg speaking about hip-hop's role in extending Beat attitudes into a new generation.

More narrowly focused exhibitions have done better jobs expanding the field: for instance, *An Opening of the Field: Jess, Robert Duncan, and Their Circle* (2014) and *Semina Culture: Wallace Berman and His Circle* (2005) explored the wide spectrum of artistic networks around these key figures. The ZKM's catalogue (2018) *Better Books/Better Bookz: Art, Anarchy, Apostasy, Counter-culture & the New Avant-garde* explores the London bookstore's "Beat counterculture" activities, including publications, art exhibitions, happenings, and support for Beats at the Royal Albert Hall's International Poetry Incarnation (1965).

The 2019 exhibition "Ted Joans: Exquisite Corpse, A Video Exhibition by David Hammons" took place at the Mau Mau/Lumiar Cité gallery in Lisbon, Portugal. There, artist David Hammons paid homage to Joans, with the first public display of *Long Distance Exquisite Corpse* (begun in 1976 and completed in 2005, two years after Joans's death). Derived from the Surrealist parlor game of the 1920s, this large "corpse" involved 132 contributors from around the world. Following Joan's initial drawing, collaborators added designs to subsequent pages of folded computer paper. Members of the Surrealists and Beats provided drawings (Roberta Matta, Dorothea Tanning, and Mário Cesariny; Ginsberg, Orlovsky, Burroughs, LeRoi Jones/Amiria Baraka, and Paul Bowles). Visual artists associated with the Beats contributed (Larry Rivers and Bruce Conner) as did jazz pianist Cecil Taylor and Hammons himself. The corpus of Joans's collaborative work was displayed in a long vitrine (reminiscent of, but an alternative to, Kerouac's *On the Road* scroll as displayed in Paris). Hammons's film about the work (2001) was projected during the exhibition. It shows Joans unfolding the artwork and artist Laura Corsiglia (Joans's companion and fellow Surrealist), who created the last drawing, describing other contributors' works.

Hammons is one of the most profound artists using and critiquing prevailing cultural and art world stereotypes. His homage to Joans suggests how future scholarship can further explore works by neglected and overlooked Beats. Hammons and the gallery—calling itself the "center for visual contamination"—frame the exhibition by employing some of Joans's favorite strategies. The exhibition's subtitle (*pela Maumaus*) suggests it was created by the anti-colonialist group Joans referenced in his famous Mau Mau costume party of 1953 (where Charlie Parker appeared as a Mau Mau) and in his poetry and collages. Joans and Hammons have always sparked dialogue and broader insight into African American contributions in jazz and other cultural forms, and Hammon's resurrection of Joans's exquisite corpse after the deaths of the Beats has propelled the Beats and Joans's works into the future.

STATE-OF-THE-FIELD SURVEY

TERENCE DIGGORY
Professor of English (emeritus), Skidmore College, Saratoga Springs, New York

With the explosion of transnational studies over the past decade, the field of Beat Studies is undergoing an expansion similar to that achieved during the 2000s by the opening of the Beat canon to include women and non-white writers. Of course, transnational studies also has an effect on the canon, by bringing attention to writers who are not American but have something "Beat" about them. But the question of what is that "Beat" something becomes focused through the transnational lens in a way that I find particularly promising. The focus is on the artistic practices that are most likely to prove useful in a different cultural context. Beatness as "lifestyle," the popular conception that continually drags on the aspiration of Beat Studies to be taken seriously, tends to get left behind in the context of the specifically American culture that gives it whatever meaning it may have. Through transnational studies, Beat writers assume their rightful place as members of an international avant-garde.

Thinking of the Beats as avant-garde artists points to future directions for Beat Studies within a national as well as transnational context. There is more work to be done on the relation between acknowledged Beats and writers identified with other avant-garde circles in the U.S., for instance Jack Spicer in the San Francisco Renaissance or Ted Berrigan in the New York School. Berrigan might provide a fresh approach to Philip Whalen, a canonical Beat writer who was a major influence on Berrigan, and who deserves more critical attention than he has recently received. Indeed, now that the canon has been expanded in terms of race and gender, Beat Studies can afford to ask what has been neglected within the "old" canon. What about Lawrence Ferlinghetti? Are we willing to take him seriously as a writer as well as a publisher and advocate? And what about non-canonical works by canonical writers? There is a great deal of material in Allen Ginsberg's *Collected Poems* that has received no critical attention because we are preoccupied with "Howl."

I offer these suggestions as prompts to stimulate critical thinking, but certainly not as prescriptions. The best of Beat Studies has always emerged, and will continue to do so, from the ability of Beat writing to grab a reader and not let go until the reader has produced a new creative response.

JANE FALK
Lecturer (retired), The University of Akron, Akron, Ohio

The current state of Beat Studies appears to be strong both nationally and internationally with a presence in conferences, a journal, membership organizations, other notable scholarly publications, and a presence in college curricula (both in survey courses and courses dedicated to writers associated with the Beat Generation). One comment here is that turnout for individual conference session presentations could be stronger. All of this points to the relevance of Beat Studies in today's culture with Beat writers still addressing social concerns of the day. Beat writers were thus prescient enough to see into the future.

My personal experience teaching such poets as Allen Ginsberg, Joanne Kyger, and Gary Snyder among others bears this out. Their work reverberates with 21st-century students, the writing more than literary artifact.

One topic of interest to me is discussion of somewhat peripheral figures who, although not part of core Beat Generation writing, demonstrate connections between the Beat Generation and other literary movements of the 1950s–1970s. One example is Stan Persky, part of the Duncan/Spicer circle and one of the editors of *Open Space* magazine. It appears that the *Journal of Beat Studies* is featuring interviews of such figures. Another topic of interest is the history/interaction of literary journals and small presses of the period where various literary strands are brought together. As well, I am interested in interdisciplinary perspectives on the Beat Generation.

AMY FRIEDMAN
Associate Professor of English, Temple University, Philadelphia, Pennsylvania

I came to Beat scholarship in the mid-1990s; I was living in London and was asked to contribute a chapter to *The Beat Generation Writers*, a British essay collection edited by A. Robert Lee (Pluto Press, 1996). I wrote about the women writers, ferreting out precious original editions of work by Diane di Prima, Bonnie Bremser, Joanne Kyger, and Lenore Kandel in archives all over that vast city. The surprising discovery that Carolyn Cassady was living in London led me quite boldly to tea and gossip, and eventually an interview, in her petite Belsize Park sitting room. That was a particularly elating period of research, but the main discovery was the interconnected way these women writers, all talented individuals, were woven into a fascinating larger picture that gradually revealed itself to be about many of the pressing topics that continue to drive central aspects of contemporary literary scholarship and investigation: hegemonies of culture, gender politics, feminist artistic agency, and the multitudinous powers of creativity.

The study of their work is by no means done; our ongoing fascination with the women Beat writers (one can add Anne Waldman, Joyce Johnson, Hettie Jones, Janine Pommy Vega, Joanna McClure, and Rochelle Owens) is born out in the continued arrival of new dissertations and published work about them. Their full influence on later creative artists has yet to be mapped, and their transnational impacts are still to be chronicled, but these women have given us a body of writing and thought that will continue to ignite inspired new scholarship. My apprehension of the current field of Beat Studies is that it has to support work in this direction, both to expand scholarship and to honor the intersectional awareness and outcomes that such work prompts. I will remain a committed reader of work on women writers of the Beat generation.

DEBORAH GEIS
Professor of English, DePauw University, Greencastle, Indiana

Whenever I have taught my "Literature and Culture of the Beat Generation" course (which I do every few years), it has filled, with a waiting list, which implies to me that millennials are still interested in Beat Generation literature. As conference coordinator (with Ronna Johnson) of the Beat Studies Association, I regularly receive proposals to present papers on our panels at the Louisville Conference and the American Literature Association Conference, often from younger scholars—which suggests to me that graduate students and new assistant professors are still vigorously involved in creating new scholarly work in the field. What I am not seeing, however, is institutional validation of Beat Studies within the academy; it is still a marginalized area in American literature without sufficient support from the MLA, from many academic presses or journals, or from a hiring standpoint. So we are at a crossroads: the literature itself still has an active readership, but (perhaps because of the nature of the work, with its emphasis on outsider status) it has not yet received the kind of canonical acknowledgment that some other genres, periods, or disciplines in literary studies have obtained.

One reason that Beat Studies is so exciting is that even though extensive work in the field (particularly biographical scholarship) already exists, there is always more to be done. Moving forward, I would especially like to see more of the following. (1) Scholarship on or about African American Beat writers that goes beyond the writers and topics that tend to be addressed (e.g., Baraka/jazz) in many different contexts. (2) More interdisciplinary work that focuses on the art and music of the period. (3) More interviews, while we still have the chance, with those who lived and worked and created alongside the Beats. (4) More experiments with applying exciting developments in literary theory to Beat work—for example, a recent paper on dust in *On the Road* (from an ALA conference a few years ago) applied OOOT (Object-Oriented Ontological Theory) to Kerouac; I would enjoy seeing more such creative scholarship.

TIMOTHY GRAY
Professor of English, City University of New York, Staten Island, New York

This past decade, I shifted a lot of my focus to music writing, publishing a book on roots rock Americana, and essays on similar topics. I maintained ties with literary studies, though, and thus view American pop music and Beat literature in a different light. I fondly recall that Bob Dylan received honorary Beat status in Ann Charters' indispensable anthology, *The Portable Beat Reader* (1992), but know now that other rock musicians, such as Janis Joplin, Patti Smith, Tom Waits, Rickie Lee Jones, Kim Gordon, Jay Farrar, and the Hold Steady, have also carried the Beat torch. Notable in this context is the back-to-back appearance of *Just Kids* (2009), Patti Smith's bittersweet memoir of becoming an artist, and *One Fast Move or I'm Gone* (2010), a documentary film based on Kerouac's despairingly gorgeous *Big Sur* (with an original score performed by indie rockers Jay Farrar and

Ben Gibbard). Both texts reinforced a message I heard Tom Waits utter two decades prior in the offbeat Jim Jarmusch film *Down by Law*: "It's a sad and beautiful world." Today, that's the phrase echoing in my head as the Beats break through and wield their unruly, holy power. The challenge, I tell myself and my students, is to forge a creative and meaningful life in such a world.

Regarding the current status of the Beats in the literary arena, I will say that I was excited recently to read *Crowded by Beauty*, David Schneider's loving and informative biography of Philip Whalen. I only wish there were more high-profile biographies of Beats not named Kerouac, Ginsberg, or Burroughs. I certainly believe that Joanne Kyger deserves a biography, or at least a book-length study. I'd say the same about Janine Pommy Vega or John Wieners (is he Beat?), or about the myriad female Beat writers who have published well-received memoirs (see Mary Paniccia Carden's recent book, *Women Writers of the Beat Era*, for incisive profiles), but whose stature would increase with a literary biography. Though I have not read it, David Calonne's new book on Diane di Prima seems like a step in the right direction. Perhaps I've missed others.

I'd also like to see a fresh appraisal of the Beats and classical literatures (both Eastern and Western), or the Beats and mythology, informed by new theoretical scholarship. As cutting-edge as Beat literature seemed in its heyday, it frequently reached back to a distant past for models of mindfulness and becoming. Whether it was Gary Snyder tapping Ovid, or Diane di Prima reading Milarepa, there existed among the Beats a thorough love of what was "gone": not only what was hip (as contemporary slang had it), but also what had vanished, awaiting a second act. Moving beyond any single author's relationship to ancient literatures, scholars of Beat literature could explore more generally the impulses driving the Beats as a group to revisit classical texts, alternately parsing reactionary or progressive aspects of this trend.

OLIVER HARRIS
Professor of English, University of Keele, Keele, Great Britain

The variety and quality of book publications in the field over the past few years is very impressive, above all with significant developments in inter- and transnational criticism from single-authored studies (e.g. Jimmy Fazzino's 2018 *World Beats*) to edited collections (e.g., *The Routledge Handbook of International Beat Literature* [A. Robert Lee, 2018] and *Beat Literature in a Divided Europe* [Henri Veivio, 2019]). The state of play therefore looks healthy. But on its own terms, I wonder if the academic roots of Beat Studies go from university press publications down into the blue-chip journals and major institutional departments, or indeed whether that's what matters. It's no bad thing that the original deep ambivalence in Beat culture towards its audience—speaking from the margins and not to the mainstream—is reproduced in Beat Studies. Just as the little magazines and small presses were more vital to Beat culture than the big publishing houses, so too in Beat Studies there should be more life outside than inside the academy.

STATE-OF-THE-FIELD SURVEY

So maybe it's a mistake to measure the state of the field according to how well it matches other academic area studies, their protocols and agendas. Maybe it's the differences and singularities that are more valuable, such as the spate of recent work on Beat music, or the consistent combination of the critical with the creative. The performative dimension has always seemed to me integral to almost everything described as Beat writing. That has had its risks—most obviously, of merging literature with life at the expense of the text itself and rigorous attention to scholarship—but it should also be a spur to experiment.

From that point of view, the book publications or journal articles are absolutely necessary but not sufficient because they aren't the best representatives of the field's health. Important as they are, they're the least able to reach new readerships and to innovate in terms of form; which is a roundabout way of saying that content per se is not the issue. The *Journal of Beat Studies* plays a key part in a field where engagement and experiment are as crucial as diversity and quality, so that the challenge is to reach out beyond borders as well as do good work within them.

ALLEN HIBBARD
Professor of English, Middle Tennessee State University, Murfreesboro, Tennessee

Beat Studies today is exciting and vibrant. We are now in a position to look back with appreciation and build on work done by pioneering Beat Studies scholars such as Jennie Skerl, Ann Charters, Nancy Grace, Ronna Johnson, Tony Trigilio, Tim Hunt, and many others. Studies such as *Girls Who Wore Black: Women Writing the Beat Generation* (by Ronna Johnson and Nancy Grace, 2002) have expanded the Beat canon, drawing our attention to contributions of writers whose work has often been marginalized. And works such as *The Transnational Beat Generation* (edited by Jennie Skerl and Nancy Grace, 2012) and *World Beats: Beat Generation and the Worlding of U.S. Literature* (by Jimmy Fazzino, 2016) have productively brought global and transnational perspectives to bear on Beat Studies.

Recent developments in Burroughs studies (to which I've been most connected) show the range, quality, and vitality of Beat scholarship. We are all in debt to Oliver Harris for his careful and meticulous textual work, as well as his now classic book *William Burroughs and the Secret of Fascination*. Michael Bolton's *Mosaic of Juxtaposition: William S. Burroughs' Narrative Revolution* (2015) deploys narratological and phenomenological theories to provide us with a better understanding of how readers interact with Burroughs' narratives. Chad Weidner's *The Green Ghost: William Burroughs and Ecological Mind* (2016) looks at Burroughs through the lens of eco-criticism. Casey Rae's *William S. Burroughs and the Cult of Rock 'n' Roll* (2019) productively explores Burroughs' profound effect on music legends such as the Beatles and David Bowie. The anthology *Cutting Up the Century*, edited by Joan Hawkins and Henry Alexander Wermer-Colan (2019), is a truly amazing collection of photos, texts, and essays. Yet another edited collection, *Burroughs Unbound*, is reportedly in the works. Meantime, Burroughs symposia, celebrations, and conferences in Mexico City, Paris (*Naked Lunch@50*), and Bloomington, Indiana, have been spectacular events, with film, performance art, music, and revelry. Another, in London, to celebrate his Cut-Ups, is planned for later this year. It has been a moveable feast, an on-going party, totally hip & cool.

The Beats were all about energy, literary innovation, movement, crossing boundaries, and critique of dominant political and social power structures. In keeping with this spirit, I hope that the field of Beat Studies will remain open to new trends and vectors of exploration, to yet unforeseen connections and new ways of composing literary criticism. The worst thing that could happen is for Beat Studies to become stale and stodgy, unreceptive to change. Like the field of literature and theory, it should be inclusive, open to a range of approaches, including (but not limited to) textual scholarship, cultural and gender studies, historical and biographical work, pedagogical issues, intertextual and interdisciplinary work, and global, posthuman (perhaps even intergalactic!) perspectives. I like to read about writers or works I've not known much about, or new takes on familiar themes and works. Keep it fresh and lively!

TIM HUNT
Professor of English (emeritus), Illinois State University, Normal, Illinois

Perhaps one way to assess the current state of Beat Studies is to recall that a half century ago no one would have thought to use the term Beat Studies. Beat writers and their work were sociological symptoms, and in that not so long ago (yes, some of us remember back that far) literary studies wasn't yet transformed into theory or cultural studies or studies of material culture or gender studies. It was still *Whoopie ti yo yo, get along little iamb,/ My clever scansion will be your new home*, and the High Church elders still insisted on the divinity of T.S. Eliot, even if new critical orthodoxy was starting to give way to something called Structuralism, with Deconstruction around the corner in the alley having a smoke. Why has Beat Studies emerged as an area of study and why is it continuing to grow richer? One (but far from the only) reason may be that the non-conformities of Beat life styles, the commitment to writing the self back into literature, and the commitment to exploring new modes of expression register more fully and richly with the critical approaches that have emerged in recent decades.

In spite of the vitality and currency of Beat Studies there is, perhaps, at least one aspect of Beat work that hasn't received the attention it might. A few years ago I asked a group of publishing students whether a book of literature was a textual object, a stored textual performance, or a transmission of a textual performance. They all simply knee-jerked that publishing was a matter of producing a textual object. Prior to the advent of recording and radio, that would be the obvious answer.

STATE-OF-THE-FIELD SURVEY

After the advent of e-books, blogs, streaming, etc., it is even less the obvious answer. The Beats were, I'd suggest, acutely attuned to the impact of then-new media and modes of mediation, not simply as content (aka pop culture) but as new rhetorics of relationships. Kerouac didn't simply write fast, he reconceptualized the medium of writing. The varieties of textual experimentation across the work of the Beats were in part an attempt to craft and perform an engagement to their era by breaking through rigid formalisms that no longer registered as authentic, but they were also a series of attempts to make writing valid and vital by connecting it to new media technologies. The way digital media are now further altering our mediascape can (and should) make the array of experimental textualities of the Beats even more apparent to us and perhaps, as well, a focus worth engaging more fully in the coming years.

ERIC KEENAGHAN
Associate Professor of English, State University of New York, Albany, New York

Identifying as a Modernist studies scholar, I feel a bit like an interloper here. My specialization actually means I'm not sure what any literary field is. In Modernist Studies, period boundaries no longer make sense and national boundaries are willingly forsaken, as our attention veers evermore toward the long twentieth century and transnational or global traditions. Even the old standard that modernism is an aesthetic formation premised upon stylistic difficulty and formal experimentation is less significant these days, as many modernist scholars increasingly study cultural texts and contexts, commercial literature, and revolutionary agitprop.

Are Beat authors part of the nebulous modernist constellation? Most definitely. Donald Allen characterized them as members of "a strong third generation" of an American modernism, thus continuing the line of writers including Ezra Pound, H.D., William Carlos Williams, and Louis Zukofsky. Yet, many of their contemporaries often positioned them as outliers, sometimes even portraying them as frauds interested more in market appeal or facile forms of social rebellion than formal experimentation. Self-identified late modernist writers, especially, took up arms, publicly and privately disclaiming the Beat phenomenon and its supposed representatives: elders not at all personally attached to the Beats, like Muriel Rukeyser; one-time mentors and sometime advocates, such as Kenneth Rexroth and William Carlos Williams; other New American Poets like Robert Duncan and Denise Levertov; and even younger writers once or later associated with the Beats, like LeRoi Jones/Amiri Baraka, Michael McClure, and John Wieners.

Our studies should try to counter sectarian divisiveness—both actual and mythological, both historically articulated by twentieth-century artists and currently in practice by some academics. That divisiveness has enabled prejudices, allowing some to feel justified in their refusal to attend Beat writing closely or actually listen to the writers' own expositions of their intentions. Critical approaches exploring the evolving connections and relations between Beat-adjacent writers and their predecessors, contemporaries, and (historically speaking) followers—as part of a modernist continuum, or a "long modernism" running throughout the twentieth century—are needed. If their contemporaries were most dismissive of Beat art for its social or political potencies (or, in the cases of writers like Baraka and Levertov, for its supposed political impotencies), then we should begin with a revaluation of those claims. Let's look closely at the work itself, its responses to and receptions within its social, political, and aesthetic contexts.

We go deeper into our own dark age, when progressive and revolutionary politics seem less viable, when global warfare and ecocide are certainties, and when social justice struggles for disenfranchised populations are increasingly fractured and weakened. The Beats' third-gen modernism could help us discover in the fabric of the present the as-yet unimagined potential for life's continuance. More simply put, the Beats are just one part of a historical assemblage of modernist artists and activists who used art, in various ways, to engage and confront existential, political, and social crises. Thus, they could help us imagine what now is literally unimaginable: a future.

A. ROBERT LEE
Nihon University, Tokyo (retired), Murcia, Spain

It would be hard to think that there has been any perceptible slow-down in Beat literary scholarship or conferencing. But both American and international readerships clearly persist, proof positive not only of ongoing interest but relish. Beat authorship assuredly remains news that stays news to adapt Ezra Pound. *On The Road*, "Howl," *Naked Lunch* all remain relative best-sellers. Film is plentiful, be it *On The Road* (2012) or *Kill Your Darlings* (2013). Documentaries range beyond J.K., A.G. and W.S.B. as usual suspects. Think of *Wholly Communion* (1965), *Wow! Ted Joans Lives* (2010), *Love Always, Carolyn* (2011), *The Poetry Deal: A Film About Diane di Prima* (2011), *The Beat Hotel* (2013), or *Big Sur* (2013). Archives grow like that in process at Naropa. Established Beat scholars have shown little let-up. The critical anthologies continue (Asher, Skerl, Grace/Skerl, Belletto).

The one lacuna may well be how much Beat writing is actually being taught. Kurt Hemmer assures me that it is still rare to meet Beat courses in the USA. Yet I've seen evidence of Beat teaching in a number of U.S. universities (indeed taught one myself at Berkeley in succession to that of Ron Loewinsohn). One step would be to get a survey done of just how many, and where, Beat courses exist. Let me add that I also know of Beat courses being taught in the U.K., France, Scandinavia, Spain, and Taiwan.

As to the authorship itself can it be doubted that Beat's women authorship is now in the picture (Knight, Peabody, Grace/Johnson, Pantano, Forsgren, Carden, Castelao/

STATE-OF-THE-FIELD SURVEY

Carbajosa)? Or African American Beat (Harris, Lee, Sollers)? Or transnational Beat (Grace/Skerl, Tytell, Bill Morgan, Fazzino, Harris/Mackay)? Or studies of Beat visual arts—photography, painting, gallery and museum exhibitions, cinema and music (Amram, Warner)? Or Beat and gender (Marler, Knight, Friedman, Damon). Beat and popular culture remains a draw (Pekar, Bokris, Cherkovski, Cottrell, Mortenson). Other Beat-inflected names have won attention (Clausen to Matson, Cohen-Jones to Townsend). My own effort in *The Routledge Handbook of International Beat Literature* (2019) was to recognize Beat writing in other Englishes and languages.

In sum, Beat and post-Beat (Meltzer, Dalachinsky, Lee) both at home and abroad is well in evidence. BSA (plus *JBS*) and EBSN and the arising print and website publications leave no doubt (Kevin Ring's *Beat Scene* invites mention). Favorites come and go, though Kerouac has rarely been out of sight. Right now Burroughs and the cut-up aesthetic rides high in the charts. An Anne Waldman, ruth weiss, or Ed Sanders performance each stirs undoubted enthusiasm, plaudits.

Beat, to be sure, rightly has to earn its imaginative keep alongside other literary-scholarly focuses—postmodern, say, or eco-centered. There also continues to be "canonical" condescension towards its texts and associated visual, musical, performance and other art. However, Beat has anything like left the stage. Quite the contrary.

HASSAN MELEHY
Professor of French, University of North Carolina, Chapel Hill, North Carolina

As someone whose home field is European Renaissance studies, I've paid close attention to recent scholarship linking Beat writing to the history of Western literature. One doesn't have to read far into the work of most Beat authors to discover a wealth of literary references: Kerouac cited Proust and Rabelais as models; he was struck by Burroughs's intelligent quotation of Shakespeare soon after their first meeting; Corso carried on dialogue with Shelley; di Prima has addressed Dante and medieval French poet François Villon; Ginsberg expressed deep affection for Rimbaud and Shakespeare. These references aren't a mere showcase of erudite credentials, but rather an affirmation of belonging to Western literature. Given the time when most of the Beat authors were educated, the 1930s to the 1950s, at issue is world literature from a Western perspective — a perspective Kerouac, Snyder, Ginsberg, di Prima, and others tried to broaden by looking to, among other areas, Buddhism, the work of medieval Chinese poet Hanshan, and the Haiku tradition founded by early modern Japanese poet Bashō.

The two pieces of scholarship I will address present Beat writers as developing their own literary identity through dialogically rewriting Western forebears. The first is an article, "Tangled Generations: Dylan, Petrarch, Kerouac, and the Poetics of Escape," by Renaissance comparatist Timothy Hampton (*Critical Inquiry* 39, summer 2013, pp. 703–31), reprised as chapter four of Hampton's *Bob Dylan's*

Poetics: How the Songs Work (Zone, 2019). By the "poetics of escape," Hampton understands writing through which authors extricate themselves from generational identity. He explains that Petrarch — if not the inventor of the sonnet, its most influential perpetrator from the fourteenth to the seventeenth centuries — waged a generational conflict with his predecessor Dante. Kerouac replays this conflict, according to Hampton, with respect to the Beat Generation: for example, in *On the Road* the beatific name Sal Paradise evokes Dante, and the woman who finally gets Sal off the road is named Laura, the same as Petrarch's love object. Dylan, dissatisfied with being the voice of his generation's protest, wrote "Tangled Up in Blue" in seven sonnet-like verses, mentioning "an Italian poet" (apparently Petrarch, though Dylan placed him in the thirteenth century), and borrowing geographical sites from *On the Road*.

The second is a collection, *Hip Sublime: Beat Writers and the Classical Tradition* (The Ohio State UP, 2018), edited by classical scholars Sheila Murnaghan and Ralph M. Rosen. Written by classicists and modernists, the contributions address Kerouac, Burroughs, Ginsberg, Corso, di Prima, and Whalen, Beat fellow travelers Creeley, Sanders, Duncan, and Olson, patron-cum-adversary Kenneth Rexroth, and comrade-in-arms Charles Bukowski. The thread tying these authors together is their common response to the classics, a canon from which they drew inspiration and of whose cultural authority they remained suspicious, often treating the suspicion as integral to the inspiration.

I view this approach to the Beat authors as important not only because it underscores their literary engagements, but also because it reveals that their capacious understanding of Western and world literature may considerably enhance its study.

WILLIAM MOHR
Professor of English, California State University, Long Beach, California

Emphatic signals of the continued "non-assimilation" of Beat writing and criticism within the academy still exist, particularly from the MLA. Perhaps the resistance to Beat writing is at least partially provoked by its willingness to continue Whitman's "language experiment." In going forward with Beat Studies, I urge us as scholars not to take the distant past for granted. I think we have a tendency to believe that Whitman is securely part of the canon. Perhaps his position is less fixed than we assume. Therefore, I would like to see more articles on Whitman and the post-Beat, for surely those of us who regard ourselves as part of that increment are far more aware of the flaws in his ideological preferences than the Beats were.

Furthermore, I wonder if what's needed is a volume on "Teaching the Avant-Garde," or rather, a series of volumes on teaching the "avant-garde" focusing on various on-going movements, including the Beat and Language writing—as well as their "post-" iterations. In general, I would like to overhear sustained discussions of how the Beat and post-Beat complicates postmodernist critiques of twenty-first century literature and society. In general, much more work needs to be done on initiating a distinct set of poets and prose writers affiliated with the post-Beat movement who have continued maturing in the past two decades. In examining this subsequent and larger group of authors, I am interested in more articles about the Venn diagram of Surrealist and Beat poetics. Part of teaching the "avant-garde" should involve a recognition of the commitment of a fairly large group of poets as well as visual artists to Surrealism, and both movements could benefit from a critical intermingling.

One challenge in the next two to three decades might be to find ways to be part of a hybrid ensemble of approaches without diluting our primary interest. What would it mean if we were to form more public alliances, and link up with scholars in queer studies or those who are more concerned with Confessional poetry or loose schools of maverick poets. I may be accused of special pleading for my own region, but there has to come a point where a West Coast canon is brought to bear on all of these topics.

Finally, in addition to more research on women Beat writers, I would appreciate more recognition given to the Beat role in the United States in calling attention to Buddhism, in addition to queer studies.

ERIK MORTENSON
Writing Center Consultant and Literary Scholar, Lake Michigan College, Benton Harbor, Michigan

From its beginnings, Beat Studies has been driven by a tension. When the Beats burst onto the postwar scene, they were viewed as both a literary and a social phenomenon. In a bid for academic legitimacy, Beat Studies has tended to neglect this social aspect, instead focusing on Beat lives and works in order to convince skeptics that the Beats are indeed serious writers whose texts warrant further study. As numerous monographs, scholarly articles, and journals such as this one amply attest, that struggle has been largely successful. Yet this emphasis on the literary has meant that equally productive social and cultural questions often go unexplored. Beat writing is not only stylistically dynamic, but addresses a range of topics and concerns that have direct relevance for our daily lives. To some extent this shift towards the social has already begun. Revisionist accounts have appeared that critically examine Beat treatments of gender and race, and a recent "turn" towards the transnational has helped place the Beats into wider global contexts. But there is much more work to be done. We have been slow to address the Beats' continuing social relevance or to bring Beat works into dialogue with today's pressing problems, despite the fact that contemporary readers still look to the Beats for answers to life's larger questions. Focusing on the social does not mean eliding texts, but rather examining how they are produced, marketed, disseminated, evaluated, and most importantly, used by readers to do cultural work.

I propose that Beat Studies take a closer look at the reception of the Beats, particularly in our present moment. Who exactly is reading the Beats? Which Beats are being read and why? What are readers doing with these works? How are the Beats being reproduced and what does this mean for how they are perceived and read? We do discuss these sort of questions, but usually informally and anecdotally. This call for a more sustained turn to reception also includes the important question of Beat influence. We have done a good job chronicling those writers and artists immediately influenced by the Beats. But what about those influenced by the Beats today? What is the Beat legacy going forward? Many Beats saw their work as not just literature, but as a blueprint for social action. Are Beat texts still viable in this sense and, if so, how so, by whom, and under what conditions?

These questions can also be thought through the negative. Why, for instance, do some Beat texts remain neglected despite their relevancy for current issues and concerns? Focusing on reception has the added advantage of allowing us to reflect on our own discipline, historicizing Beat Studies to reveal how it has helped shape our understanding of the Beats as objects of inquiry. This survey is itself an important step in that direction.

DARIN PRADITTASANNEE
Assocciate Professor of English, Chulalongkorn University, Bankgok, Thailand

To my understanding, the field of Beat Studies has attempted to interrogate the meanings of "beat" and "Beat writing" as well as the distinctive features of the Beat movement and Beat aesthetics in the context of America in the 1950s and 1960s. The field expands its canon from an emphasis on white male figures such as Kerouac, Ginsberg, and Burroughs to include women Beat writers, writers of color, and writers of ethnic minorities. There has been the examination of Beat writings in relation to other art forms and their connections with other literary movements, such as modernism. The field has also benefited from various theoretical perspectives, such as feminism, postmodernism, and queer studies.

The directions of Beat studies could be influenced by new issues in contemporary society. Such topics as the new conceptualization of human identity and society as impacted by science and technology may be brought to bear in the re-examination of Beat writing. As the world is facing environmental crises and has witnessed species extinction, ecocriticism and animal studies could be used as lenses to shed different light on Beat literature.

Transnational perspectives on Beat writers and their cultural production could be one of the field's main focuses. Several Beat writers travelled or lived abroad; for instance, Kerouac in Mexico, Ginsberg in India, and Snyder in Japan. I am interested

STATE-OF-THE-FIELD SURVEY

in reading the historical studies of individual Beat writers' literary and/or spiritual journeys to those countries, which trace places that they visited, include interviews with the locals who had interactions with the writers, and analyze the writers' portrayal of those places. One important issue is the Beats' interactions with, and possible influence upon, local writers/thinkers. One could also interrogate how the Beat writers' sense of self is altered in their contact with the Other. In other words, the studies of Beat literature in global contexts may help us better understand the issue of self and the Other, especially the possible blurring of self-other boundaries and the re-conceptualization of self and the notion of Americanness.

Another phenomenon in contemporary society is the movement of the younger generation ignited by their revolutionary spirit, as evident in the protests in Hong Kong or the powerful influence of environmental activist Greta Thunberg. As our younger generations' activism and rebellion are reminiscent of the spirit of the Beats who questioned the mainstream culture and its norms and revolted against an amoral, hypocritical society, it would be fascinating to read critical works which make transnational, trans-temporal connections between the Beats' counterculture movement and the protest movements of younger generations in our times. It could be the study of the rhetoric deployed by these individuals/groups of different time periods. Finally, one salient phenomenon—both in America and my country, Thailand—is that our younger generations face depression and mental disorders. Their psychological problems parallel the frustration and dejection of the post-war generation of the Beats. When comparatively examined, the predicaments of these different generations could illuminate each other.

ROSEANNE QUINN
Instructor, De Anza College, San Francisco, California

The current state of Beat Studies is a thriving and energized one. I have noticed at several conferences, for example, a renewed interest in the Beats coming particularly from graduate students and junior faculty. The field has further broadened its trajectory in terms of approaches globally and from transnational perspectives. That does not just involve U.S.-based scholars following the Beats on their "worlding" journeys, to borrow Jimmy Fazzino's phrase. But accessibility to Beat literature also continues to develop as the literature appears in translation for readers outside of the U.S. The contributions of scholars such as Spanish feminists Isabel Castelao-Gómez and Estíbaliz Encarnacíon-Pinedo have enlivened feminist approaches and extended the reach of European Beat Studies.

The future of Beat Studies is vast and promising. On the one hand, its relevance to today's sociopolitical movements and modes of cultural consciousness are ripe for connection. In terms of my own interests, I am revisiting di Prima and what we can see in her works as early articulations of the #MeToo Movement within current multi-valent feminist politics—amid her Italian American cultural affiliations with Italian-descended San Francisco Beat poets. The interdisciplinarity of the field historically, combined with the efforts of younger scholars to re-think Beatness itself, has created avenues for my own work that keep me coming back and keep me challenged.

It would further enrich the field to continue to examine how current writers, who are shaping cultural critique right now, can be studied within a Beat context. There is an ongoing future in, say, pairing the work of Fred Moten—with his critical and poetic theorizing and articulations on musicology and the Black imaginary—to re-invigorate previous Beat scholarship and widen our ongoing understanding of the contributions of writers of color, race and racism in the Beat era, the Black Arts Movement, Black Lives Matter, and beyond.

In terms of the *Journal of Beat Studies* (*JBS*), it is the ongoing mentoring by its editors of younger scholars, intersectional scholarship, and the Beats' connections to non-literary art forms, such as painting, drawing, various forms of studio art, as well as popular culture. As the vocabularies of intersectional lenses are already in development, I also value the further study of categories of sexuality and gender across fluidity, non-binary spaces, and trans voicing to exploring newer ways to discuss the real lives of the Beats as expressed narratives of non-heternormativity.

It is important still to ground Beat scholarship in pedagogy. After all, the Beats were also great teachers, founded schools of thought and verse, and continued much valued collaborations with each other. That is why new work such as the forthcoming anthology on Beat literature and the classroom is so important.

Finally, there are Beats still traveling among us, such as di Prima and Anne Waldman, who, as with all great teachers, and in true Beat spirit, remind us that the revolution is in our movement forward.

ELENA ROGALLE
Doctoral candidate, University of Central Florida, Orlando, Florida

The field of Beat Studies has many strengths. First, the writers are still cool. In my experience, it's easier to get undergraduates to read Beat literature than Keats or Pope, but what I find lacking on syllabi are the women writers—despite the resurrection and attention paid to their work over the last twenty years. This absence creates a hole in the history of the Beat Generation as well as American history.

Another weakness is lack of interdisciplinary scholarship. Interdisciplinary work can help broaden the audience for Beat Studies. The stories of these women writers would be a perfect transmedia narrative. In the chapter "Searching for the Origami Unicorn," Henry Jenkins states: "a transmedia story unfolds across multiple media platforms, with each new text making a distinctive and valuable contribution to the whole. In the ideal form of transmedia storytelling, each medium does

STATE-OF-THE-FIELD SURVEY

what it does best." Using hypertext, the narratives of these women would unfold through a website.

To further enhance the narrative, Story Maps—which combine maps with narrative, images, and multimedia content—can be used to create world building. For instance, a hyperlink from the website to the story map could be embedded in the website. A VR experience could also be created taking viewers into the Cedar Bar in the 1950s to experience the sounds and sight of that space using vintage footage of Beat writers performing their work.

In my research for my dissertation at the University of Central Florida, I am using Omeka web application to develop a digital bibliography to make searching and finding women Beat texts more readily available. Each entry will make searching for texts by women Beat writers easier. By developing the database, a foundation is created that can lead to future projects such as a digital archive, mobile apps, and other future digital media.

DAVIS SCHNEIDERMAN
Professor of English and Krebs Provost and Dean of the Faculty at
Lake Forest College, Lake Forest, Illinois

I think the field is highly specialized—like many others—and always risks gradual obscure obsolescence as time passes beyond the lifespan of the surviving participants. The danger is even more in Beat Studies due to the somewhat biography-focused "fanboy" aspect of the field, as received by much of the general public. Therefore, I agree that the most productive areas are to explore intersections with some of the areas you note above in your questions, and to broaden the impact (and the canon) even further.

It seems essential to further globalize the field, and to trace its influence through the movements and artists who trace some aspect of lineage to the "core." I'd like to read direct overlap as much as possible with self-critical explorations of the current limit of Beat Studies—what can it not imagine yet, but should—and how can it demonstrate its relevance to the current moment. In Burroughs studies, for instance, there is a text waiting to be written on the links between his theories of media manipulation and the current state of our fraught internet culture (deepfakes, etc.).

JOHN SHAPCOTT
Honorary Research Fellow at Keele University, Keele, Great Britain

Given the quantity, quality, and range of hard copy and online Beat material being produced, there is every reason to be optimistic. The challenge now is to demonstrate the relevance of our work to the wider polity whilst building links between academic and popular communities of Beat enthusiasts. This involves continuing to bring Beat women participants in from the cold, expanding research on gender and race, being prepared to accept open, but well monitored, artistic borders allowing us to welcome otherwise marginalised figures into the field ....Above all, it seems to me, there is a great responsibility to show that Beat Studies has a role to play in the debate over climate change, to become an aesthetic, social, and political constituent of Extinction Rebellion.

Beat ecology remains a neglected research field, which is odd given the strong ecopoetical Buddhist bent of so many writers, notably Ginsberg, Snyder, McClure. The recent publication of Chad Wiedner's T*he Green Ghost: William Burroughs and the Ecological Mind* should prompt us to be innovative in our readings of other Beat writers, researching their intertextual links, and examining their possible influence on public policy makers. How strange that Kerouac's texts still await the deserved close ecological exegesis that could, for instance, take *The Dharma Bums* out of backpackers' pockets and into the current climate debate on wilderness and species loss.

Edward Abbey's *Desert Solitaire* stands with Kerouac's *Dharma Bums* and *Desolation Angels* as a firsthand engagement with wilderness—both authors wrote books based on journals kept while working for the National Park Service. In a similar vein, T. C. Boyle's work deserves recognition in Beat Studies, as shown in a recent issue of *Beat Scene*, a publication bridging the academic and the popular.

Simon Warner/Jim Sampas's and Casey Ray's published ventures into Beat's affiliations with rock music suggest a wide field inviting further research, one that would be helped by making available such tapes as Ginsberg's reading of *Mexico City Blues.* Classically inflected Beat compositions currently receive little attention—Philip Glass, Kronos Quartet, Enno Poppe are representative candidates. The latter's Interzone, for example, situates Burroughs's collaged city voice in a tradition going back to Baudelaire.

Publication remains the canonical life-blood of any discipline and here we have to address the question of who will publish and at what price. The withdrawal of Southern Illinois University Press from Beat publications is unfortunate. Is the answer in part more paperbacks like A. Robert Lee's 2019 *The Beats: Authorship, Legacies* (Edinborough UP), competitively priced? At some stage, starting with Kerouac and Burroughs, there need to be fully annotated uniform critical editions of their variant texts.

STATE-OF-THE-FIELD SURVEY

Resident in England, I would welcome comprehensive digital scans of otherwise difficult to access Beat papers, such as those held at the New York Public Library. At a stroke, this would forward world-wide research whilst meeting an obligation to cut our carbon foot print.

JENNIE SKERL
Associate Dean of the College of Arts and Sciences (retired),
West Chester University, West Chester, Pennsylvania

A once-neglected field, Beat Studies has grown to maturity in the depth and breadth of scholarship devoted to the many writers (and other artists) who identified as Beat; or who were linked to the Beats by affinity, publications, or other venues; or who claim the Beats as models or forerunners. One of the most important developments in Beat scholarship has been the recognition of authors whose contributions were initially overshadowed by the fame of a few popular icons—not only contemporaries of Kerouac, Ginsberg, and Burroughs such as John Clellon Holmes and Brion Gysin, but also younger second and third generation writers such as Ed Sanders and Anne Waldman. Once perceived as a group of three to six white males active in the 1940s and 1950s, the Beat Generation has now been reconceptualized as a diverse group of men, women, races, ethnicities, genders, sexualities, and generations spanning the 1940s to the 1970s and beyond, and generating an art style that has influenced artists across multiple genres and media. The recovery of Beat women writers has probably been the most important part of the reconfiguring of the field, attracting the attention of scholars and critics beyond Beat Studies itself. This turn in Beat scholarship was initiated by Ronna Johnson and Nancy Grace. A second important development has been a focus on the transnational character of Beat writing in the work of American authors and writers around the world. A transnational perspective highlights the global circulation of Beat poetics and the existence of parallel movements. Exploration of transnational Beat Studies was addressed early by A. Robert Lee, Jaap van der Bent, and myself—and continues apace.

The *Journal of Beat Studies* has been crucial to the field in publishing articles meeting the highest standards of scholarship, interviews, and other primary materials, a generous serving of reviews in each issue, and an annotated index of new publications. All of these contributions are key to the establishment of Beat Studies as a respected field of study. The editors defined the journal in issue #1: "Our mandate is to provide readers with intelligent and penetrating criticism across the range of Beat writing, including fiction, poetry, drama, autobiography, life writing, and screenplay writing. The ultimate goal of the journal is to advance the quality of Beat Studies scholarship through application of diverse critical perspectives and address Beat production as both complex art and cultural critique." The journal is successfully carrying out its purpose, and, in particular, I urge you to continue to publish reviews, since no other source reviews Beat scholarship regularly or extensively.

KATHARINE STREIP
Associate Professor of English, Concordia University, Montreal, Quebec, Canada

There has been exciting new work in Beat Studies in the past six years: Beat Generation literature as a global phenomenon, transnational approaches to Beat literature, gender, posthumanism, ecology, Beat drama, the Beats and philosophy, Beat writers and the classical tradition, as well as exciting work on individual authors—Oliver Harris's invaluable annotations to Burroughs's cut-up trilogy, J. C. Cloutier's work on Jack Kerouac's French writing, Tony Trigilio's collection of Elise Cowen's poetry, Veronique Lane's work on the French genealogy of Beat writers. However, even though it is clear that young people are interested in Beat writers, there is still reluctance by universities to accommodate that interest. One of my former students entering an M.A. program was discouraged from working on Jack Kerouac, reminding me of how graduate students were steered away from "feminist" topics in the '80s. I'd like to see more courses offered on Beat writers at the undergraduate and graduate level, from a variety of perspectives: historical, literary influences and antecedents, aesthetics, critical race theory, queer theory, ecocriticism, affect theory, sound studies, spirituality (religious studies, magic and esotericism), addiction studies, anarchism and libertarianism, feminism, avant-garde movements, cultural criticism, psychoanalytic criticism/dream work, media studies. For innovative approaches to Beat writing, it is important to support young scholars and give them encouragement and a platform for their work.

Beat Studies publications should be focused on a broad range of approaches and high quality scholarship and writing. The field should be eclectic and adventurous, inspired by the spirit of Beat creators.

TONY TRIGILIO
Professor of English, Columbia College Chicago, Chicago, Illinois

During the past few decades, Beat Studies has created a legitimate disciplinary space for itself without sacrificing the experimental artistic and intellectual energy that draws so many of us to Beat writing in the first place. We all can be proud of our field's accomplishments in just the past three decades alone: terrific scholarly monographs and book-length essay collections; outstanding scholarly articles; insightful conference programming from an international network of two vibrant scholarly organizations, the Beat Studies Association and the European Beat Studies Network; and a near-decade of important work published in our field's academic journal, the *Journal of Beat Studies*.

We have produced a significant body of scholarship during the past three decades, and the quality and quantity of this scholarly production has honored the work of prior scholars who often risked their academic reputations to study Beat writers and artists. Unfortunately, I still encounter literary scholars outside our field who believe the facile academic stereotype that Beat literature is either not substantial enough for serious scholarly study or that Beat literature is too hip to be understood by the aesthetic, historical, and theoretical scholarly practices reserved for other movements and writers. The friction between Beat Studies and official academic culture is partially a result of the historically conflicted relationship between Beat writers themselves and academic institutions. The Beats were a different breed, and that's why many of us were drawn to them. With this in mind, Beat Studies is best served by scholarship that explores the uniquely innovative aesthetics of Beat Generation writing and art without fetishizing this uniqueness and without, in turn, lowering our standards for historical and theoretical readings of Beat texts and contexts.

I'm encouraged to see less hagiography as the field grows and that biographical criticism is being deployed more as a foundation for substantive discussion of Beat works and their historical contexts rather than as an end in itself. Scholars in other literary fields approach their work with a commitment to close, detailed readings of primary texts themselves, and to the historical contexts, and power dynamics, of the production and reception of these primary texts. As the field of Beat Studies has grown, I am glad that Beat Generation literature is being approached in much the same way, balancing an appreciation for the uniqueness of the Beats with our ongoing commitment to rigorous scholarly methodologies.

I'd like us to continue working from critical perspectives that explore questions of power in Beat writing (especially race, class, gender, sexuality, and postcolonialism) and that also examine the transnational production and reception of Beat work. I continue to be intrigued by the possibilities of confronting head-on the relationship between Beat writers and the academy. Substantive work is in progress, I know, on the tension between Beat countercultural impulses and the bureaucratic pressures of academic institutions, and our field would benefit from more research and writing on this subject.

SIMON WARNER
Visiting Research Fellow, School of Music, University of Leeds,
Leeds, Great Britian

Beat Studies, in the context of Europe and by extension the U.K., seems to be in good health, judging by the continued success and expansion of the European Beat Studies Network and its annual conference. My live presentations on the Beats in bars, libraries, and festivals in the last 18 months have also proved a good audience draw. Again, in a purely anecdotal sense, my own University of Leeds class, "Joined at the Hip: Rock, Jazz and the Beat Generation," was a popular and over-subscribed course among undergraduate students over the 10 years it ran. By implication, the field that interests me most—Beat's relationship to music—seems also to have secured a place in this wider scholarly terrain, particularly post-Millennium. In that period, writers such as Lewis MacAdams, John Leland, Laurence Coupe, Simon Warner, Nancy Grace, Casey Rae, and others have built on the work of earlier pioneers like Barry Miles, Steve Turner, Holly George Warren, and Stephen Ronan, who focused on the way the Beats responded to music or how musicians responded to the novels, poetry, and ideology of the writers. The areas of concern have tended to focus upon the relationship of this literary community to styles that fall broadly under the heading popular music: jazz, an elastic descriptor embracing Hollywood ballads to unrestrained free music with so much in between, and rock, in its many post-mid-1960s incarnations. A monograph on Kerouac and jazz is in preparation by Marian Jago. There are multiple further ways in which the connection between the Beats and musical expression/practice could be further investigated, a point to which I return below.

Some thoughts on areas in that Beat/music nexus could be explored further: (1) A potentially fascinating area of consideration is that between what A. Robert Lee has called "the Afro-Beats" and the hip hop and rap formations that have become ubiquitous in global music since the 1970s. There are lines of connection between figures such as Leroi Jones/Amiri Baraka, Ted Joans, and Bob Kaufman, political and artistic radicalism in the 1960s, and the emergence of Gil Scott Heron, the Last Poets, and others in the chain of major African American writer/performers of the last 50 years: from Grandmaster Flash to Public Enemy, Michael Franti to Arrested Development and Mos Def/Yasiin Bey, and on to contemporary figures like Robert Glasper and Kendrick Lamar. A forensic enquiry into this genealogical line between the black Beats and the music makers and wordsmiths of today would be valuable, and a book-length study is overdue. (2) The original Beats' interest in orchestral and symphonic music, styles falling outside the popular axis, would also make for revealing research, I think. (3) There is, too, so much more we need to know about jazz and Beat (e.g., jazz poetry, Rexroth, weiss, Ferlinghetti, Meltzer, Waldman, and more recent figures like Steve Dalachinsky) and rock and Beat (e.g., Meltzer again, King Crimson, Dana Colley, Death Cab for Cutie, Ben Gibbard/Jay Farrar).

REVIEWS

The Green Ghost: William Burroughs and the Ecological Mind
By Chad Weidner
Southern Illinois University Press, 2016

Chad Weidner's innovative study of William Burroughs as an ecological writer comes at an opportune time amidst the increasingly anxious and politically fractious debate about global warming, loss of habitat, and species extinction. Weidner is critically scrupulous in unpacking all of Burroughs's major texts, in published chronological order, within the context of environmental literary criticism. This inclusiveness matters because whereas it is relatively easy to make the case for the two late works *Ghost of Chance* (1995) and *The Cat Inside* (2002) as ethical ecological novellas that deal imaginatively with the difficult intellectual challenge of how to conceptualize non-human agency, the early works present something of a deeper ecopoetical theoretical challenge. Weidner meets this challenge head-on in his discussion of *Naked Lunch* (1959) in which he shows how the biosphere—air, water, plant, and animal life—open up a radical meta-contextual ecocritical perspective beyond conventional inherited modes of thought.

Weidner's introductory material usefully draws attention to the proliferating number of contemporary ecocritial texts, while helpfully placing them in the context of those prescient historical nature writings that pleaded for a greater understanding of the human impact upon the natural world. Particularly relevant are two names not normally associated with Burroughs but whose co-option here opens up exciting new possibilities for Beat generation scholarship. The green anarchist leanings of transcendentalist Henry David Thoreau, along with his rejection of authoritarian government, are seen as the crux in establishing the real relevance of Burroughs to ecocriticism. Leo Marx's emphasis in his *Machine in the Garden: Technology and the Pastoral Ideal in America* (Oxford UP, 1964/2000) on Thoreau's realization that with old agrarian life-styles in terminal decline "the only sensible thing to do is to get off the track" because "the writer's first duty is to protect his powers of perception" (54-55), plays precisely into Burroughs's mindset of postmodern freedom.

No single distinctive methodology currently defines environmental criticism. Weidner opts for a basic breakdown of the myriad possible approaches by referring to the set of overarching "concentrations" adopted by American Studies scholar T. V. Reed: conservationist, ecological, biocentric/deep ecological, ecofeminist, environmental justice. Weidner invokes all but the ecofeminist "concentration" to a greater or lesser degree as offering what he calls a useful "port of entry" for his engagement with the present state of ecological studies, echoing the title of Robert A. Sobieszek's *Ports of Entry: William S. Burroughs and the Arts* (LA County Museum of Arts, 1996). Alongside an introduction to current ecocriticism, Weidner also selects some of what he sees as the centrally important, often innovative, critical studies of Burroughs, beginning in 1971 with Eric Mottram's seminal *William Burroughs; The Algebra of Need*. Two major subsequent Burroughs studies are referenced, namely Timothy Murphy's *Wising Up the Marks: The Amodern William Burroughs* (1997) and Oliver Harris's *William Burroughs and the Secret of Fascination* (2003), neither of which specifically mentions ecological concerns. Weidner takes issue with Murphy's dismissal of Burroughs as a revolutionary writer, arguing rather that *Naked Lunch's* toxic warnings signal it as radically prescient. But his study is more sympathetic to Harris's belief that "attention to the materiality of textual production can offer exciting possibilities to exploring ecological concerns" (Weidner 9).

Weidner's chapter on *Naked Lunch,* "Burning Bones: The Limits of Material Culture and the Toxic Human in *Naked Lunch*," introducing the notion of toxicity as a significant and recurring trope in Burroughs's texts, nods towards Harris's methodology. The seemingly unlikely figure of the drug addict becomes a metaphor for environmental pollution through toxic exposure to narcotics, as well as introducing the idea of general societal behavioral guilt through self-contamination, whether through the use of domestic plastics at the micro level or air travel at the macro level. But it is the big corporations that are most severely indicted for constructing a system that by putting profit before ecological purity creates, in Weidner's words, "an economic system in crisis" (25). He identifies what I regard as a central ecopoetical passage in the novel, warning of an ecosystem in crisis: "A vast still harbour of iridescent water. Deserted gas well flares on the smoky horizon. Stink of oil and sewage. Sick sharks swim through the black water, belch sulphur from rotting livers, ignore a bloody broken Icarus" (Weidner 25; Burroughs, *Naked Lunch* 64). Weidner makes a compelling case for reading Burroughs as a writer whose ecological time-span links classical to contemporary times via the figure of Icarus, who represents the "pride and vanity of a naive and youthful industrial nation soaring to high but brought back low" (26). As Weidner's argument progresses, this time-span begins to take on even more ecological significance as he considers Burroughs's excoriating take on the colonial degradation of native natural resources with no thought for either inhabitants or nature. In contending that this toxic dystopian scene is "significant in showing points of intersection between economics, society and the environment" (25), Weidner demonstrates a readiness to engage with what environmentalist Thoreau first coined as *extra-vagant* (*Walden* 216) and to wander beyond established boundaries. The issues raised soon reach the limits of any one intellectual discipline, making *Naked Lunch* a fascinating case study of an unstable text open to a critical universe of multiple readings, from Marxism to posthumanism.

It is with the textually short but ecocritically important *The Yage Letters* that Weidner widens his exploration of Burroughs's critique of Western postcolonialism and environmental justice, using the term "biopiracy" to define Western exploitation of natural resources in areas of South America. More importantly, however, in terms of his positioning Burroughs as an ecological writer, is his referencing the fragmentary nature of *The Yage Letters* to alert us to the *Nova* trilogy's experimental use of cut-ups as a dynamically progressive proto-ecological aesthetic form. In so doing, Weidner raises questions about how we adapt ecocritical arguments to pressing postcolonial issues.

The very aleatory, unconventional form of the cut-up is seen as allowing for new ways of viewing literature that have the potential to recover otherwise suppressed elements of environmental meaning. Even so, the encounter between postcolonial thinking and ecocriticism in *The Yage Letters* has an unfortunate habit of taking on the coloration of a neocolonial text as Burroughs/Lee consistently describe South American citizens "as a race of dirty and diseased prostitutes and hustlers" not to be trusted (Weidner 41). It would be productive to read Burroughs's condemnation of Western oil exploration in the South Americas alongside a writer who gets a fleeting mention from Weidner. While Edward Abbey admittedly writes from the Beat margins, he also shares something of Burroughs's eco-vision. Abbey's *Desert Solitaire* (1968) argues for the preservation of wilderness for political reasons, "as a refuge from authoritarian government, because history demonstrates that personal liberty is a rare and precious thing" (130). In passages that suggest the perfect terrain for Burroughs's *Wild Boys*, Abbey points to the existence of wilderness as a haven for revolutionaries, a base for guerrillas to mount effective resistance to totalitarian regimes.

Weidner's extended discussion of the cut-up technique centers upon *Nova Express* which, 50 years since first publication, is now considered more relevant than ever. Faced with the seemingly insoluble problem of the safe disposal of toxic waste, *Nova Express* becomes a handbook, in both form and content, for green anarchism. It challenges boundaries between nature and cities, inverting the pastoral by describing landscapes that are antagonistic to sentimental expressions of home and hearth. We are invited to read Burroughs as a committed political literary eco-warrior calling for a global struggle against minority controlled capitalist interests and structures that assume an automatic right to run the planet in their own interests. Weidner's contention that the *Nova* trilogy "is constructed from the rubbish of existing textual discourse, so the materiality of the texts can be directly linked to a trash aesthetic" (72), while linguistically persuasive, fails to fully engage, however, with the potential of the literature of waste for a radical ecological manifesto.

The *Red Night* trilogy of the 1980s embarks upon an ambitious agenda for dismantling existing rigid structures of social and political control in favor of more fluid, adaptable, and therefore long-term sustainable forms of human society. Weidner provides a critically assured guide through Burroughs's complex narrative strategy of weaving diverse cultural and religious texts in the trilogy to create what he labels as a "retroactive utopia" (85, 95, 161). This leads readers into a fascinating area of political philosophy in which Burroughs's introduction of micro-political systems of political democracy can be historically linked to Samuel Taylor Coleridge's attempt to found a utopian colony in America, organized on the principle of the communal ownership of property, a system referred to as "Pantisocracy." It would have been helpful to have read this chapter of Weidner's book in the context of Michael Foucault's essay "Different Spaces," which develops Burroughs's notion of retroactive utopias as "heterotopias," spaces of contestation, both mythical and real. One of the principles of Foucault's heterotopias that chimes with Weidner's view of the cut-ups as mutable forms is their ability to juxtapose in a single real location several emplacements that are seemingly incompatible in themselves.

There is an aesthetically satisfying ecopoetical circularity as we reach the conclusion of *The Western Lands* (1987), one that returns to the central environmental concern of *Naked Lunch*, the now even more pressing threat of a toxic universe. Burroughs's consistency of moral and political viewpoint over some 30 years stakes an impressive claim:

> I want to reach the Western lands—right in front of you, across the bubbling brook. It's a frozen sewer. It's known as the Duad, remember? All the filth and horror, fear, hate, disease and death of human history flows beneath you and the Western Lands. Let it flow! My cat Fletch stretches out behind me on the bed... (257)

The appearance of Burroughs's cat Fletch anticipates and provides the link to one of Burroughs's slimmest but intriguingly provocative and challenging texts. *The Cat Inside* raises issues distinct from writing about ecosystems, pollution, and power structures. Weidner's chapter ventures into new territory in Burroughs critical theory, looking at animal ethics as concerning the animal as an individual existence, to be considered as having equal value to a person. He is aware that "anthropomorphic writing is not the straightforward application of human characteristics to nonhuman creatures" (122), placing Burroughs's description of close relationships with his feline companions within a phenomenological or hermeneutic network of meaning within which a cat experiences and orientates itself. This sets up the most controversial section of Weidner's critique in which the proposition that for a cat to kill is natural raises the unanswered question of why the same impulse should not apply to humans. Weidner admits that Burroughs fudges an issue that in the novella is closely allied to his warning of species depletion/extinction. It is at this point that Weidner makes an unfortunate category error in calling as witness the "animal activist Elizabeth Costello" (134), a fellow advocate prophesying that the extinction endgame will be a silence beyond redress. Costello is not a real person, but rather a fictional character featured in J. M. Coetzee's *The Lives of Animals* (1999). In Coetzee's polemic, not cited by Weidner, his startling and controversial comparison between human concentration camps and nonhuman slaughter-houses would have made the perfect companion piece to the discussion of a novella in which Weidner rightly observes that Burroughs "asks the reader to identify not only with the death of the animal but also with the murderous human that lies within all of us" (117).

It is in Weidner's discussion of Burroughs's late novella, *Ghost of Chance*, and the confrontation of old world romanticism with the ethics of the non-human animal that a Burroughs text is seen to formulate pressing environmental dilemmas in a form readily accessible to the general reader. *Ghost of Chance* represents an alternative heterotopian historical account of an attempt by a group of reformed pirates to establish a libertarian state. Their leader, Captain Mission, is set on building a sustainable society capable of finding a balance between civilization and nature. The revelatory aspect of this text is the extent of Burroughs's sheer love of animals and his fear for their survival in an exploitative capitalist system. The looming sad fate of Burroughs's Madagascan lemurs shows yet again environmental criticism poised on the pressing but difficult intellectual question of how to conceptualize non-human agency. Beyond the scope of Weidner's study, Burroughs's paintings warrant critical exegesis for their experimental abandoning of representational visual expectations in favor of a radical, associative, tempered abstraction that often critiques industrial/military practices that are environmentally damaging. Particularly telling is his 1965 collage *The Energy of a Hurricane* that references the Esso logo amidst the destruction in the hurricane's wake. Lemurs appear to be the great survivors, close to Burroughs's heart, as they frequently emerge unscathed and beautiful from the chaotic abstraction surrounding them: *Wood Spirits* (acrylic, india ink, paper on plywood with shotgun holes), *Black Lemur 30,000 Years Old* (paint and offset lithography on paper), and the stunningly beautiful *Brightness Falls from the Air* (paint on wood and glass window). All these pictures may be found in the Los Angeles County Museum of Art's 1996 volume, *Ports of Entry: William S. Burroughs and the Arts*. One of the many virtues of Weidner's well-researched and ground breaking study is that it encourages the Beat scholar to explore this previously neglected visual art side of Burroughs's output, and so widens the scope of critical exchanges in Beat ecocritical culture.

The Green Ghost makes a welcome addition to what remains a severely restricted field of studies devoted to the Beats and the environment—to date, the main contenders are Michael McClure's *Scratching the Beat Surface* (North Point Press, 1982), Rod Philips's "*Forest Beatniks*" *and* "*Urban Thoreaus*": *Gary Snyder, Jack Kerouac, Lew Welch, and Michael McClure* (Peter Lang, 2000), John Suiter's *Poets on the Peaks: Gary Snyder, Philip Whalen & Jack Kerouac in the North Cascades* (Counterpoint, 2002), and Jason M. Wirth's *Mountains, Rivers, and the Great Earth: Reading Gary Snyder and Dōgen in an Age of Ecocritical Crisis* (SUNY Press, 2017). The challenge now is not only to widen the field of Beat writers, including formerly marginalized Beat women writers, within the critical outreach of environmental criticism, but to focus in analytical detail on the texts of specific individuals. Weidner's in-depth analytical study of Burroughs as an environmental writer is, in this context, a pioneering literary and cultural study that bodes well for the future development of Beat ecopoetics.

—John Shapcott, University of Keele

Works Cited

Abbey, Edward. *Desert Solitaire: A Season in the Wilderness*. Robin Clark, 1992.
Burroughs, William S. *Naked Lunch: The Restored Text*. Grove, 2001.
---. *The Western Lands*. Picador, 1987.
Thoreau, Henry David. *Walden and Civil Disobedience*. Norton Critical Edition, 1966.

Straight Around Allen: On the Business of Being Allen Ginsberg
By Bob Rosenthal
Beatdom Books, 2019

Bob Rosenthal moved from Chicago to New York in 1973, encouraged by poets Ted Berrigan and Alice Notley to join a thriving Lower East Side poetry community in which Berrigan and Notley were key figures. New York was "a veritable badlands" for Rosenthal, where he endured "[p]erpetual siren screams and stinking garbage in the streets" for the sake of a "poet's promise of no career and no money" (4). But the possibility of a career in poetry changed dramatically for Rosenthal when he accepted a job as Allen Ginsberg's secretary in 1977, becoming "the low-paid secretary to a Bardic Poet whose life's work is a cottage industry run out of an apartment by poet cultural workers" (19). He would hold this position until the poet's death in 1997.

Tensions between poetry and commerce are central to Rosenthal's memoir of his two decades in the Ginsberg office, *Straight Around Allen: On the Business of Being Allen Ginsberg*. As Rosenthal soon learned after taking the position, his primary job was to maintain the infrastructure of the Ginsberg "cottage industry," an aesthetic and commercial enterprise that promoted Ginsberg's career while also serving as a central location for literary community organizing on the Lower East Side. "The cottage industry model means caring for the workers. In our case the industry is Allen," Rosenthal writes. "Poetry is the cottage that contains us. Poets get jobs to help other poets" (26). In this way, the book is also a tribute to a New York in which poets could afford (albeit marginally) to live. Rosenthal remembers mid-1970s New York as a city "peppered with survival work opportunities that don't pay much. Working at the Strand Bookstore. Reading books on tape for the blind. Proofreading. The city only offers enough to live in it" (38). The Ginsberg office was a vital part of such an environment. It was a space where "Allen hires poets to do real work. Allen provides them with a needed income" (26).

Although he started the job as "the low-paid secretary to a Bardic Poet," Rosenthal quickly became a trusted member of the poet's inner circle and eventually part of Ginsberg's chosen family. This level of intimacy serves the book well. Rosenthal's Ginsberg is a study in contrasts: a visionary poet also preoccupied with the business of literary reputation; a serious Buddhist who also hovers near the telephone when Rosenthal takes calls; a benevolent boss providing employment opportunities for young artists and one who also plays favorites, especially with male workers in the office; and an artistic role model whose attraction to interpersonal chaos threatens the stability of a loosely structured office environment. This is not just another Beat memoir that trades off short-lived encounters with the movement's most well-known writers, such as Sam Kashner's *When I Was Cool: My Life at the Jack Kerouac School* or Trevor Carolan's *Giving Up Poetry: With Allen Ginsberg at Hollyhock*. Rosenthal's book is an intimate account by a writer who organized Ginsberg's professional life and also helped coordinate the poet's peripatetic personal life—the writers, musicians, and fans endlessly passing through Ginsberg's apartment—and was there at the end, among those compassionately caring for the poet during his last days.

The unique structure of Rosenthal's memoir reflects the clash of voices and personalities that characterized day-to-day life in the Ginsberg office. The primary text of the book is flanked on the margins with remarks and anecdotes (in a different typeface and reduced font size) that create a continuous dialogue with the book's main narrative. The text in the margins offers explanatory detail, as one might expect, for instance, from footnotes; however, the marginal text strategically competes with, and interrupts, the primary text. The result is a deliberate entanglement of narratives that, taken together, enact the dialogic environment Rosenthal was responsible for managing in the Ginsberg office. Rosenthal's conversational structure self-consciously disrupts the linearity of conventional narrative with unpredictable associative leaps and tangents—surplus material that narrative cannot fully account for—all of which enact a fuller, more experiential understanding of the multi-tasking unruliness that was a vital creative presence in an office that was as much a clerical space as it was an atelier.

Still, even as the book's engrossing anecdotes in the margins de-center narrative authority, they also risk an elision of the unflattering elements of the Ginsberg mythos. A notable example is Rosenthal's discussion of Ginsberg's misogyny. Observing that he "met many women who will never forgive Allen for his brusque treatment towards them," Rosenthal concludes, "I naively call him [Ginsberg] a benign misogynist" (28). But the running commentary on misogyny in the margins includes a necessary corrective from Barbara Barg: "I use 'benign misogynist' to poet Barbara Barg and am quickly chastened, 'Well, that sounds like an oxymoron, doesn't it?'" (28). As if in response, the primary text defers to euphemism and rings of defensiveness: "Allen transforms gender into self," Rosenthal writes. "He does use a feminine form of intelligence in his poetry. His sexual expression is structured to engender a feeling of liberation. Allen finds the key in the window" (28-29). To be sure, Rosenthal's final sentence, his appropriation of the words of Ginsberg's mother, Naomi, from "Kaddish" ("'The key is in the window, the key is in the sunlight in the window'"), is a significant reminder that Ginsberg's friendships and relationships with women were shaped in part by his lifelong effort to make meaning from his mother's mental illness and death (*Collected Poems* 232). However, these remarks from Rosenthal in the primary text require running commentary in the left-hand margin for the most complete critical context; there, on the periphery rather than at the center, Rosenthal adds his own self-corrective response: "The oppression of women stems from all forms of men: straight and Allen's nearsighted gayness!" (29). Rosenthal's dialogue between the narrative margin and center is an innovative strategy to construct a nuanced understanding of the artistic and political complexities of the Ginsberg industry. At times, however, Rosenthal's negotiation of the margin and center reproduces the same hierarchical division that the book's unique structural form seems designed to erase; in such instances, candor itself—"straight and Allen's nearsighted gayness!"—risks being relegated to the political margins.

Such collisions of purpose between homage and critical prose occur just enough that the book might at times produce hesitation in scholarly readers. Scholars will have to sift through anecdotes that function more as appreciatives in order to piece together the most complete account of life in the Ginsberg office from 1977-1997. All the same, it is important to emphasize Rosenthal's effort to craft a delicate balance between homage and critical prose, as in the considerable detail Rosenthal devotes to the difficulties Ginsberg faced in managing the chaos of his personal life—social tumult that, all the same, served as a pattern of influence in Ginsberg's poems. For most of Rosenthal's two decades as secretary, the physical boundary between Ginsberg's home and office was almost non-existent; located in two adjoining Lower East Side apartments, home and office inevitably encroached upon each other. Home and office were governed by a "chaotic atmosphere of people wandering in and out through the rooms," which, as Rosenthal notes, was "Allen's way of making a home. It is fundamentally communist from aesthetics to practice" (7). Rosenthal's narrative offers an important reminder of the extent to which the poet's childhood contributed to this chaos. "Kaddish," a foremost example, dramatizes the young Ginsberg functioning in an impossible dual role as both son and caretaker for Naomi as her illness worsened. *Straight Around Allen* demonstrates how Ginsberg normalized this psychic disjunction as an adult. Rosenthal crucially reprints verbatim a letter he wrote to Ginsberg during the poet's 1984 tour of China, documenting Peter Orlovsky's violent breakdown, and subsequent arrest, while Ginsberg was away. Orlovsky's arrest is a matter of public record and has been discussed in Ginsberg biographies by Barry Miles, Michael Schumacher, and Bill Morgan. However, the full version of Rosenthal's letter to Ginsberg, included in its entirety in *Straight Around Allen*, provides extensive detail and immediacy unique to an unedited item of personal correspondence. The events depicted in the letter, triggered when Orlovsky threatened the office staff with scissors and a butcher knife, affirm that day-to-day life in the office suffered from Ginsberg's excessive tolerance for destructive behavior (often by Orlovsky). In the letter to Ginsberg, Rosenthal pleads, "Now Allen, from what I can see and what I have learned—you are in classic role of THE ENABLER it is a role that must stop not only must you not give PO [Orlovsky] money to drink (establish trust fund?) but you will have to examine your part of the total equation I.E. how do you get your hook out of PO" (86). Ginsberg's attraction to personal turmoil can be seen throughout his body of work; not only in the Naomi triptych (the poems "White Shroud" and "Black Shroud," in addition to "Kaddish"), but also in Ginsberg's tributes to his first Tibetan lama, Chögyam Trungpa Rinpoche, a brilliant teacher who helped bring Tibetan Buddhism to North America, and a heavy drinker capable of authorizing the violence narrated in Ed Sanders's *The Party: A Chronological Perspective on a Confrontation at a Buddhist Seminary* and Tom Clark's *The Great Naropa Poetry Wars*. The Ginsberg cottage industry was built on a psychic fault line, and it was from this seismic stress that his most successful poems were composed. Chaos, Rosenthal writes, is "the only sort of home that he [Ginsberg] knows" (22).

One of the major strengths of this book is its suggestion, not emphasized enough in Ginsberg scholarship, that Ginsberg identified almost as much with teaching as he did with writing. *Straight Around Allen* is filled with anecdotes in which Ginsberg runs the office as both benevolent boss and attentive pedagogue. Ginsberg's identity reflected that of a patient teacher as much as it did, for example, the canny, self-conscious media figure more familiar to readers in poems such as "Ego Confession." Even during his final hospital stay, Ginsberg was teaching. On the last weekend of his life, as Ginsberg was wheeled on a gurney into Beth Israel Hospital's emergency room, an ER doctor slipped him a poem for critique. Later, meeting with his cardiologist, Ginsberg gave back the poem with his handwritten editorial notations. "He [Ginsberg] asked the doctor to return it to the ER physician," Rosenthal writes. "She was surprised and said, 'That was kind of rude of that doctor.' Allen broke into a self-satisfied smile and said, 'I made it a much better poem'" (152).

Rosenthal's touching account of the poet's final days offers invaluable biographical detail for scholars. As he does with his 1984 letter to Ginsberg, Rosenthal reprints verbatim his extensive diaristic notes on those last days, which were among the research materials Morgan incorporated in his 2006 biography, *I Celebrate Myself: The Somewhat Private Life of Allen Ginsberg*. The unedited version of Rosenthal's account reproduced in its entirety in *Straight Around Allen* offers crucial insight into the extensive literary community Ginsberg constructed over the years, a chosen family that complemented his biological family. Rosenthal's narrative of the poet's last days also provides additional information on the enduring effects of Ginsberg's lost childhood. Meeting with Ginsberg's hepatologist, Dr. Clain, as the poet is dying, Rosenthal urgently explains Ginsberg's medical history to Clain, emphasizing in particular the poet's botched childhood appendectomy and subsequent infection. After examining the appendectomy scar, Clain asks, "'So, Mr. Ginsberg, this happened when you were a child?' […] 'Oh No!' Allen piped up, 'I wasn't a child. I must have been ten!'" (152). Similarly, Rosenthal's detailed rendering of the day Ginsberg died can move a reader to tears. It is a compelling account of the passing of a literary celebrity in prose that eschews the trappings of celebrity. His narrative of those last days reflects the stark honesty of Ginsberg's final poems of illness, and loss of body functionality, in *Death and Fame: Last Poems, 1993-1997* (reprinted in the *Collected Poems*). It is a communal death, the poet surrounded by friends, family, and his teacher, Gelek Rinpoche, who gathered a group of monks to chant and prepare Ginsberg for the death process. The parting words of Ginsberg's older brother, Eugene, who would die four years later, are heartbreaking: "Good night Little Allen. I'll see you soon" (156).

Memoir, by its nature as a genre, cannot replace critical biography for the knowledge it makes about its subject. But memoir's intimacy, the emotional knowledge that it creates and the archival detail it provides, can be a significant component of scholarly research. *Straight Around Allen* offers important insight into the day-to-day particulars of the Ginsberg industry, including the extent to which commerce and poetry competed against each other for Ginsberg's attention (despite the decidedly noncommercial, vatic lineage from which his poems emerge). Rosenthal describes Ginsberg as someone "so loved and feared that people hold their peace around him and wait for him to leave before falling apart" (22). What is unique, and ultimately valuable, about *Straight Around Allen* is Rosenthal's perspective as an intimate witness to the turbulence that was the Ginsberg industry's center of gravity.

—Tony Trigilio, Columbia College Chicago

Works Cited

Carolan, Trevor. *Giving Up Poetry: With Allen Ginsberg at Hollyhock*. The Banff Centre, 2001.

Clark, Tom. *The Great Naropa Poetry Wars*. Cadmus Editions, 1980.

Ginsberg, Allen. *Collected Poems: 1947-1997*. HarperCollins, 2006.

Kashner, Sam. *When I Was Cool: My Life at the Jack Kerouac School*. HarperCollins, 2004.

Miles, Barry. *Ginsberg: A Biography*. HarperCollins, 1989.

Morgan, Bill. *I Celebrate Myself: The Somewhat Private Life of Allen Ginsberg*. Viking, 2006.

Sanders, Ed, editor. *The Party: A Chronological Perspective on a Confrontation at a Buddhist Seminary*. Poetry, Crime, and Culture Press, 1977.

Schumacher, Michael. *Dharma Lion: A Critical Biography of Allen Ginsberg*. St. Martin's, 1992.

Approaches to Teaching Baraka's Dutchman
Edited by Matthew Calihman and Gerald Early
Modern Language Association of America, 2018

When Amiri Baraka's play *Dutchman* was produced in 1964, it marked a moment of personal, literary, and social transition for the playwright and for society. At the personal level, the work signaled Baraka's distancing from the Beat bohemians he associated with and his movement toward Black Nationalism, a shift he would ultimately mark by divorcing Hettie Jones, his white wife, changing his name from LeRoi Jones to Imamu Amiri Baraka (he later dropped Imamu), and moving from Greenwich Village to Harlem before eventually returning to his native Newark, New Jersey. At the aesthetic/literary/social level, the work proved seminal in the developing Black Arts Movement as a way of expressing impatience with social change through the Civil Rights movement and an insistence that Black people should define their own cultural stance and aesthetics, and take charge of their own liberation/condition. The new volume *Approaches to Teaching Baraka's* Dutchman, published by the Modern Language Association (MLA) as part of its well-known Approaches to Teaching series, offers perspectives from professors and teachers at several universities on how to approach teaching this work that, as the back-page blurb puts it, "continues to speak to racial violence and inequality today." Regarding the editors, Matthew Calihman is an associate professor at Missouri State University. His publications include "'Where Are the Italian Anarchists?': Amiri Baraka and the Usable Pasts of the Immigrant Left" (*Voices in Italian Americana* 2007) and "Black Power beyond Black Nationalism: John A. Williams, Cultural Pluralism, and the Popular Front" (*MELUS* 2009). He is a co-editor of a special issue of American Studies devoted to Ralph Ellison (2015). Gerald Early is Merle Kling Professor of Modern Letters, professor of English, and chair of the African American Studies Department at Washington University. He has published *A Level Playing Field: African American Athletes and the Republic of Sports* (Harvard UP 2011); *This is Where I Came In: Black America in the 1960s* (U of Nebraska P 2003); *The Culture of Bruising: Essays on Prizefighting, Literature, and Modern American Culture* (Ecco Press 1994); and *One Nation Under a Groove: Motown and American Culture* (Ecco Press 1995; U of Michigan P 2004).

This book has two main sections as well as a preface; the book also contains notes on the contributors, a bibliography of works cited, an index arranged by name of person referenced, and a list of "Survey Participants" representing respondents to a survey used by the volume's editors "as they conceived this volume's introductory essays" (181). The "Preface" provides a general cultural overview of the period in which Baraka wrote the play, as well as of some of the intellectual and cultural influences that lie beneath Baraka's work, and gives a brief biography of Baraka through the 1960s, including his separation from the Beats, his founding of the short-lived Black Arts Repertory Theater/School, and his emergence as a leader in the Black Arts and Black Power movements. Part One, "Materials," lists respectively biographical and autobiographical materials pertaining to Baraka; books, edited collections, and special issues of journals devoted to Baraka and his work; early productions of *Dutchman*; works, interviews, archival materials, and other sources that provide context for the publication and reception of *Dutchman* and its place in the social milieu of its time, including the bohemian and avant-garde scenes; *Dutchman's* significance in light of the Black Arts Movement of the 1960s and 1970s; *Dutchman's* "intertexts," meaning its intersection with myths or works by authors, musicians, and artists ranging from Dante and Wagner to Ralph Ellison and Richard Wright; and mention of the two main editions of the play (which bear slight differences) as well as collections of works by Baraka. Part Two, "Approaches," contains essays by academics on methods and strategies they have used in approaching and teaching Baraka's play and forms the body of the work.

The three subsections of the "Approaches" part, "Performing Identities," "Dramatic Histories," and "Cultural Interplays," present various strategies for teaching *Dutchman*, with the fullest development coming in the "Cultural Interplays" part. "Performing Identities" approaches the play from the angles of creative writing, cinema, and the context of international production. Andrew Ade's essay "Teaching *Dutchman* Through Creative Writing" describes pre-reading and post-reading approaches to orient students toward the issue of racial confrontation that is central to the play by having students write about people stereotyping each other or "exhibiting 'offensive' or 'taboo' public behavior" (29), or in post-reading scenarios having students reimagine a scene by reversing the race or gender roles of the characters. Ade emphasizes that creative writing can "facilitate learning and self-reflection" while defusing "feelings of trepidation or hostility toward Baraka's vision" (25). Katarzyna Jakubiak's "Teaching *Dutchman* from an International Perspective" brings new light to the play by emphasizing how the play can be reconfigured to address cultural issues in an altogether different social context. Specifically, productions in communist Poland involved blackface performance that Polish actor Maciej Englert described marking "difference" generally rather than race (see pp. 44-45). William Thomas McBride analyzes the play through its film version (Dir. Anthony Harvey, 1966), emphasizing framing shots, use of soft focus, and other cinematic techniques that heighten or illuminate aspects of the drama, and discussing how these effect the interpretation of the play. Of the essays in this section the one by Jim Cocola seems weakest; Cocola uses the metaphoric construction "in the round" to view the play from multiple perspectives. As he puts it, "To teach *Dutchman* in the round is to encounter a confrontational text in a setting that fosters dialogue" (34). But the concept becomes so diffused that it comes to include everything from having students play parts in class to having the teacher dress like a character from the play. While the essay offers numerous pedagogical approaches to the work, its overuse of the phrase "in the round" leads to confusion, especially considering that theatre in the round conventionally refers to deployment of a central stage surrounded by audience space, making the concept more architectural than panoptic.

"Dramatic Histories" highlights the work in view of its literary and social contexts. Meenakshi Ponnuswami's "*Dutchman* in the Drama Class" argues for a "triply historicized approach" (69) that views the work from 1) the social context of the era in which it appeared, including documentaries, writings on theatre by Baraka and others, and contemporaneous white liberal perspectives; 2) Modernist influences including those of the Absurdist Edward Albee and the French theorist Antonin Artaud; and 3) other theatrical representations of race from such writers and playwrights as James Baldwin, Ntozake Shange, August Wilson, and in film, Spike Lee. Daniel Morris ("Baraka's Aesthetic Radicalism: *Dutchman's* Modernist Roots") traces Modernist tendencies and influences in Baraka's work, exploring its archetypal qualities as "the expression of a modernist mythopoetic imagination" (74). Kurt Hemmer ("Breaking from the Beats: Teaching *Dutchman* as a Critique of Black Nationalism") reads the play in relation to Baraka's transition from the Beat scene into Black Nationalism, while Matthew Calihman ("*Dutchman* as Black Avant-Garde Historical Drama") situates it in the tradition (if the word is appropriate) of avant-garde theater tracing back to Dadaism, and more directly in relation to a "black Dada" Baraka imagined stemming from "the avant-garde jazz of Ornette Coleman [and its] aesthetic scourge on white supremacy" (86). Deborah M. Mix ("Culture and Violence in *Dutchman* and the Black Arts Movement") locates the play within the Black Arts movement to examine the play's explorations of relations between violence and art. She interestingly also discusses the relationship between the Black Arts movement and the "double message" (95) of popular Motown hits of the era such as Martha and the Vandellas' "Heat Wave" and "Dancing in the Streets." Koritha Mitchell ("What's Love Got to Do with It? Everything! Teaching *Dutchman* and 'The Revolutionary Theatre'") considers the play in light of Baraka's essay "The Revolutionary Theatre," first published in 1965, to confront the seemingly contradictory "objects of love" in the play, arguing that students' "search for these objects provides an invaluable framework for *Dutchman*" that allows the class "to acknowledge the role of love in Baraka's theory" which is expressed as "black female energy," disguised though it may be by a "masculinist conception of power" (97-98).

The subsection "Cultural Interplays" largely involves comparative analyses of intersections of cultural features in the work in an effort to provide insight into some of the contextual elements framing Baraka's play. Andrew Sargent's "'Free of Your Own History': Implicating Students in *Dutchman*" focuses on presenting *Dutchman* as a play still relevant to students today since it warns that "it may be impossible to escape America's tortured racial history" (106). "Reading *Dutchman's* Setting" by Richard Schur considers the play's setting in a New York subway car in relation to African American historical interactions with trains both symbolic and real, such as the Underground Railway, the history and mythology surrounding black laying of railroad track (exemplified for instance in the tale of John Henry), the Pullman Porters, and other interactions between Blacks and railroads in American culture. In "*Dutchman*, the Black Body, and the Law," Danny M. Hoey, Jr. explains how his initiation to the work ultimately led him to teach it "to help students understand how the Black male body is constructed as violent and angry" and how this fact "elicits the real violence often perpetrated against it" (123). "*Dutchman's* Uncle Tom" by Tess Chakkalakal approaches *Dutchman* by reading it in light of Harriet Beecher Stowe's *Uncle Tom's Cabin* and the permutations the character of Uncle Tom has undergone since the publication of Stowe's work, arguing that Baraka's play "constitutes a dramatic response to the history of white stage adaptations of *Uncle Tom's Cabin*" (128). Roland Leander Williams, Jr. ("*Dutchman, A Raisin in the Sun*, and the History of Minstrel Theater") posits the minstrel tradition of American theater as establishing a "theatrical convention" (134) of Black stereotyping that both Baraka and Lorraine Hansberry in *A Raisin in the Sun* work against. In "*Dutchman* and Black Vernacular Culture," Jean-Philippe Marcoux works from the perspective of the African American vernacular, defined by Henry Louis Gates, Jr. and Nellie Mckay as "forms sacred — song, prayers, and sermons — and secular — work songs, secular rhymes and songs, blues, jazz, and stories of many kinds" as well as "dances, wordless musical performances, stage shows, and visual art forms of many sorts" (qtd. in Marcoux 140) to show how, in the play, the character Clay "employs black vernacular culture to confront the history of race relations in the United States as well as the stereotypes it generated" (140). D. Quentin Miller's "'And That's How the Blues Was Born': Baraka's *Dutchman* and Baldwin's *Blues for Mister Charlie* in Conversation" compares these two plays to show how they "highlight the ambivalence and tension surrounding integration in the early 1960s" (147). Molly Hiro ("'No Metaphors,' 'No Grunts': Dutchman, Black Arts, and Authenticity") explores "discourses of racial representation and racial authenticity" in Black literary works in her African American Writers survey course, and uses *Dutchman* to provide "a new and challenging perspective on these issues" (154). James D. Bloom describes in his article "Amiri Baraka and Philip Roth: Passing, Place, and Identity" how he uses *Dutchman* to help explore "identity construction and cultural heritage" (161). As contemporaneous writers both born and rooted in Newark, New Jersey, Baraka and Roth each explore their respective ethnic African American and Jewish identities through their connection to Newark while confronting "passing," or acceptance into the dominant society, and its impact on ethnic identification. This essay provides an interesting comparison between Baraka and Roth, but I was surprised that Bloom left to the end mention that "Baraka became a flashpoint in Roth's novels," that Roth used Baraka as "a scapegoat for the loss of Newark's rough charm," and that Roth had characters in his novels refer to Baraka as "that son of a bitch LeRoi Jones" and as "a literary fraud " who "writes 'Black propaganda' masquerading as 'literature'" (167). Such details one would think would be important caveats to bear in mind when comparing these two authors — especially in light of the accusations of anti-Semitism that have been raised against Baraka. Last, Caleb Corkery, in "Teaching *Dutchman* with *Chappelle's Show*: Arguments Along the Color Line," argues that skits from David Chappelle's comedy series can help illuminate "the absurd history that creates…racialized beings" (168) that both Baraka and Chappelle explore.

Many of these essays are anecdotal, telling the story of the evolution to a teaching approach, or strategic in focus, laying out the underlying strategy of the class. Most also contain multiple references to works or artifacts the instructor can introduce or use to shed light on some aspect of Baraka's play. Aficionados of the Beats will particularly connect with Hemmer's essay on Baraka's split from this group and will also enjoy the essays relating *Dutchman* to jazz and bebop as an avant-garde movement of Black cultural expression that was, of course, also important to the Beats. Before reading this collection, I never thought of John Coltrane's rendition of "My Favorite Things" as the joyous shredding of a white cultural icon (see Jean-Philippe Marcoux's essay, "*Dutchman* and Black Vernacular Culture"). There are, of course, potential approaches to *Dutchman* that are not covered; one could imagine, for instance, a pedagogical treatment of the play from the direction of gender or queer studies that would focus on a potential shifting of gender roles in the work, perhaps influenced by issues of race. Ade's essay comes closest to this potential approach in his suggestion of using creative writing strategies to have students reimagine scenes from the play, perhaps by shifting the genders of the two main characters. Strictly structural or formal analyses also seem eschewed, except perhaps in the case of McBride's exploration of the cinematographic strategies employed in Anthony Harvey's film version of the play. No attempt is made to link the play to some sort of psychological or other form of "case study" of Baraka himself. Most approaches rely on the intersection of some cultural trend or comparative figure to provide insight into the work, perhaps on the justification that *Dutchman's* relevance needs to be restated for a generation that might like to think of itself as "post-black" or past the animosity that accompanied the 1960s struggle for civil rights. Either way, the teacher of *Dutchman* will find a wealth of suggestions and possibilities here that may shed light on approaches one can take in teaching this important play.

—Allan Johnston, Columbia College Chicago

Diane di Prima: Visionary Poetics and the Hidden Religions
By David Stephen Calonne
Bloomsbury, 2019

Despite what might appear to be a penchant for self-revelation, Diane di Prima remains elusive to many readers who are otherwise familiar with Beat writers, perhaps because of her almost trickster-like refusal of categorization or perhaps because of academics' reluctance to fully engage her canon. When di Prima appears in scholarly commentary about the Beat Generation and about twentieth-century American poetry, it is generally in pieces—parts of poems, a single text, one genre. David Stephen Calonne's *Diane di Prima: Visionary Poetics and the Hidden Religions*, the first scholarly monograph dedicated entirely to di Prima, provides a reason for the lack of more comprehensive treatment of this important literary figure *in toto*: at the risk of sounding like an undergraduate in an introductory poetry course, her work is both difficult and voluminous, shaped by a rigorous and life-long practice of self-education in hermetic traditions. Calonne's literary biography persuasively demonstrates that the complexity and density of di Prima's poetry, its evocativeness, resonances, and challenges, are rooted in complex and dense influences synthesized over the course of a life dedicated to spiritual enlightenment and discovery.

Calonne's project encompasses di Prima's "complete oeuvre" (vi) with the goal of explicating her "idiosyncratic style," which, he argues, is rooted in "visionary tradition[s] unfamiliar to many readers" (1). The book grows out of insights developed in his earlier study *The Spiritual Imagination of the Beats* (2017), which investigates the shaping influence of "hidden" religious traditions on "Beat artistic creativity" (*Spiritual Imagination* 1). His chapter on di Prima examines "disparate sources" that "nourished" a "literary imagination" formed in the belief that "being a poet meant embarking on a religious quest" (*Spiritual Imagination* 41, 37). *Diane di Prima: Visionary Poetics and the Hidden Religions* expands this line of inquiry, providing a crucial and truly illuminating lens on her canon through exploration of her self-directed studies in areas such as ancient Egyptian religion, Greek mystery cults, alchemy, Tarot, Tree of Life, Native American shamanism, Gnosticism, Kabbalah, goddess worship, Zen and Tibetan Buddhism, and the *I Ching*.

"The hidden religions" is di Prima's term, meant, Calonne explains, to reference hermetic beliefs and practices that "emerged out of a syncretism...between Greek and Egyptian thought" which later meshed with alchemic principles of "'correspondence' between the earthly and cosmic realms." "Hidden religions" further incorporates spiritual traditions that "monotheistic, orthodox faiths" deemed heretical, such as witchcraft, Gnosticism, and a number of Eastern belief systems (*Diane di Prima* 4). For di Prima, the hidden religions represent a "'secret history' of intellectual and spiritual evolution...aimed at human liberation" (178). To explore these spiritual and philosophical modes of thought, Calonne draws on many of the texts she included in the "Hidden Religions in the Literature of Europe" course she taught at the New

College of California's Masters in Poetics Program. His analyses of these texts, which he identifies as di Prima's primary influences, serve to establish their foundational role in the development of her poetics.

Previous scholarship on di Prima has generally recognized her interest in occult topics, Eastern spiritual traditions, and world mythology. Commentators routinely describe her poetry as surreal, mystical, and/or spiritually oriented. Nancy M. Grace and Ronna C. Johnson identify di Prima's interest in myth and her studies of "Zen and the magical arts" as central to her poetic practice (82). George Butterick remarks on her attraction to alchemy, medieval writers, and "mythmaking" (150), and Anthony Libby finds in her poetry a "romantic primitivism" and "blood mysticism...embedded in the mysteries of the flesh, the sacred processes of the body" (58, 50). Brenda Knight points out that di Prima taught classes in "occult and Hermetic traditions in poetry" and established a San Francisco institute devoted to "healing...and magical practice" (127). Calonne departs from earlier critical engagement with di Prima's life and literary work in two major regards. First, while many scholars who identify spiritual elements in di Prima's poetry tend to locate them primarily in her later work, especially *Loba* (1978), Calonne demonstrates that an hermetic aesthetic has underwritten her poetics from its inception. Second, although it is not unusual to see di Prima's poetry characterized as "visionary," Calonne is the first to give this term the full weight it deserves in interpretation of her canon; he thoroughly investigates manifestations and implications of her visionary quest for meaning and traces the development of her visionary aesthetic to specific philosophical, religious, and scientific sources.

Calonne's deep dive into di Prima's visionary poetics leads him in different directions from those previously taken in di Prima scholarship. For example, commentators discussing her early life routinely cite Dante (to whose work she was introduced by her anarchist grandfather) as a formative influence. While Calonne does describe Dante as one of the major "Italian thinkers and poets to whom she was exposed at a very early age," he identifies the more important figure in the evolution of her thinking as Giordano Bruno (1548-1600), "the great 'heretical' philosopher, mathematician, and theorist of the infinite universe" (17, 11). It was Bruno, he argues, who "shape[d] di Prima's...intellectual trajectory" with his view of "the poet as a kind of Magus, a 'co-creator with God,'" his belief in "the plurality of worlds," and his "heroic example" of remaining true to one's convictions (12, 23, 132). Calonne finds elements suggestive of Bruno's cosmological thought infused throughout di Prima's canon—in the first poem she wrote at age six; in work she composed in the 1950s; in *Revolutionary Letters* (1971); in later writings and lectures on literary, scientific, and spiritual topics; and in her priorities as a teacher, critic, and social activist.

Diane di Prima: Visionary Poetics and the Hidden Religions proceeds chronologically, following a general pattern in which Calonne intermeshes biographical information with detail about di Prima's reading within philosophical and religious fields. After providing explanation about the writers, concepts, and theoretical paradigms di Prima studied, he explores their impact on her literary work and draws connections to other American writers with similar interests. For example, part of his chapter "The Age of Aquarius and the Wolf," which covers 1968 through 1979, addresses her study of "Renaissance magus" John Dee (1527-1608/9), an astronomer and alchemist determined to find a means of communicating with angels. A scholar and advisor to Queen Elizabeth I, Dee, as Calonne reports, is said to have achieved the state of "mystic exaltation...much desired by the Beats" (156, 157). Calonne summarizes Dee's theories, explores di Prima's interpretation of his work in her preface to his "weird and complex text" *Monas Hieroglyphica* (1564), and analyzes poems—including "Jacob's Ladder," "John Dee," "Vector," and "Darkness Invocation/Winter Solstice 1976"—in which she uses related terms and imagery to express "spiritual yearning" for the kind of oneness posited in the "gnostic ascent to One, to God" (157-61).

Later in the chapter, Calonne points to areas of coincidence between di Prima's understanding of Dee and her reaction to the work of Henry Corbin (1903-1978), a twentieth century "French scholar of Islamic mysticism" (152), who posited an "imaginal zone"—a realm "between the 'empirical world and the world of abstract understanding'"—that "corresponds to the angelic realm" (171, 172). In addition to supporting Calonne's examination of di Prima's thinking about spiritual guides, this material also serves to illustrate his argument that her poetics and spiritual practices "integrate a variety of philosophical traditions" as a means of "heal[ing] the split between self and cosmos" (173). Dee appears again in the next chapter as part of Calonne's ongoing discussion of di Prima's interest in angels, this time in her essays and lectures on H.D. (Hilda Doolittle) in which she traces a "genealogy of angel magic" through the centuries to affirm that "poetry is magic" and that the purpose of poetry is the "drawing down of god forms" (195).

Other figures studied by di Prima range from Sir Isaac Newton to the Swiss alchemist and astrologer Paracelsus (1493-1541) to Frances Yates (1899-1981), a British historian who wrote extensively on Renaissance philosophy. As Calonne tracks di Prima's fascination with the "metaphysics of light," he explores her reading of German occultist theologian Heinrich Agrippa (1486-1535) and Robert Grosseteste (1175-1253), a medieval English philosopher whose categorizations of light appear in her 1981 poem "Studies in Light" (183-84). Di Prima's theorizing about light and her use of light in her work is one of the threads Calonne follows throughout the book; he examines permutations and incarnations of light as "symbolic of the spirit," both individual and universal (183-84, 133), and points to other Beats (Gregory Corso, Philip Lamantia, Michael McClure) who make "the phenomenology of light a continuing theme" in their literary work and in their pursuit of enlightenment (46).

Beats are known for their attraction to Eastern religions, and Calonne traces out in detail the specifics of di Prima's immersion in Buddhism—from her investigation of Zen meditative practices in the 1950s to her studies with Shunryu Suzuki Roshi (1904-1971) in the 1960s and 1970s and her subsequent forays into Vajrayana Buddhism with Chogyam Trungpa (1939-1987) in the 1980s and with Lama Tharchin Rinpoche (1936-2013) in the 1990s. Calonne examines intersections between Buddhist belief and di Prima's politics and poetics while also pointing to her facility in pulling together Buddhism with other spiritual practices. He makes it a priority to demonstrate not only that her studies gave her an erudite understanding of various traditions as they evolved over the centuries—her reading of "Renaissance occultists," he argues, led her to "a long chain of mystical thought in Germany which had its roots in ancient Neoplatonism, in Kabbalistic lore, and in the texts of Hermes Trismegistus" (154)—but also that she used her studies to create new modes of spiritual and poetic expression. For instance, he notes her "effortless syncretism in combining Hindu and Kabbalistic conceptions" in "Number Fifty-Seven" of *Revolutionary Letters* as evidence of the combined importance of a wide variety of "hidden religions" in her creation of "her own unique and individual style" (155).

Calonne does not neglect the literary figures whose influence on di Prima is likely better understood by Beat scholars, though not necessarily in the hermetic contexts in which he places them. Di Prima's regard for John Keats as her "mentor and guide" is well known (*Recollections* 162); less well known is her 1975 Naropa lecture "Light/and Keats" in which she describes him as "an initiate of the esoteric traditions" and analyzes his notion of negative capability through the Gnostic belief in enlightenment through "direct knowledge of the divine" and through the alchemic quest to "transform" the material universe "so that...spirit...fills everything" (150, 152). Similarly, Calonne's account of Ezra Pound's influence on di Prima highlights Pound's "orientation toward esoteric philosophical sources" (34), his investment in Grosseteste's view of light as "the prime form of the cosmos" (43), and his attraction to the Eleusinian mysteries and their reiteration by "troubadour poets of the Middle Ages" (42). Di Prima, Calonne argues, is "rare among American poets in her appreciation" of Pound's "hermetic knowledge" (42).

Discussions of di Prima's Beat-associated friends and colleagues reveal shared artistic priorities and common interest in, for instance, Tarot (Gregory Corso, John Wieners, Robert Duncan, Charles Olson), magic and the occult (William S. Burroughs), Hinduism (Olson), angels (Corso, Lamantia) and alchemy (McClure, Duncan). Calonne speculates that Olson might have introduced di Prima to Henry Corbin's work (171) and suggests that elements of her essay "Paracelsus: An Appreciation" echo comments made by Duncan about "the correspondences that haunted Paracelsus, who saw...that the key to man's nature was hidden in the design of the larger Nature" (100). Such observations invite further investigation of connections between hermetic tradition and Beat literary practice, perhaps, as Christopher Gair suggests in his review of *The Spiritual Imagination of the Beats*, in relation to ways in which "the hidden religions shaped the formal aspects of the writers' work" (73). I wish Calonne had gone into more specific detail in this regard; I also wish that he had afforded more than brief referenes to areas of overlap between di Prima and women such as Anne Waldman, Joanne Kyger, and Lenore Kandel.

Nevertheless, one can't help but be staggered by the amount and depth of research that went into *Diane di Prima: Visionary Poetics and the Hidden Religions*—Calonne's study incorporates aspects of literary history, works by a wide range of authors, criticism specific to the Beats and associated circles, and texts by and about theologians, scientists, mathematicians, astronomers, philosophers, alchemists, and practitioners of occult mysteries. Beyond the considerable undertaking of explicating arcane and esoteric sources spanning more than ten centuries, his project of accounting for di Prima's full canon is daunting in and of itself. Much of her poetry is out of print or difficult to locate, a good deal of her work remains unpublished, and her papers are distributed among ten university archives. In addition to her poetry, Calonne digs into her drama and fiction, her syllabi and class notes, her letters and notebooks, her published and unpublished lectures on matters ranging from H.D.'s "angelology" (192) to Italian Americans and race (212), and her essays, articles, prefaces, and introductions addressing literary, philosophical, and spiritual topics.

Unfortunately, synthesis of all of this primary and secondary material is often uneven, leading to discontinuities, abrupt shifts in thought, and unfinished lines of argument. Given the importance of Calonne's contribution to di Prima scholarship, it is possible that Bloomsbury's eagerness to see it in print resulted in hasty editing that leaves the book feeling both rushed and repetitive. A more serious drawback that should have been rectified during the editing stage is the book's mode of documenting sources; paragraphs of material drawing on a number of different texts are often accounted for in a single footnote. While this is not always a problem, in some cases it becomes an obstacle. When notes contain multiple citations, for example, it is not always clear which aspects of Calonne's claims are factual and which are conjectural, or which parts of his commentary are his alone and which are paraphrased from the work of others. Readers interested in tracking down his sources will have difficulty aligning specific elements of his argument with corresponding citations in footnotes that are occasionally comprised of 15 or more references.

Despite these frustrations, *Diane di Prima: Visionary Poetics and the Hidden Religions* is essential reading for scholars and students of di Prima and the Beats. It opens di Prima's canon in new ways and reveals fascinating lines of exchange between writers that add depth and dimension to Beat studies. The connections Calonne draws between the multiple and diverse traditions that di Prima studied, practiced, and expressed in her work illuminate elements of her poetry that might otherwise seem inaccessible. His attention to themes that extend throughout her long career implicitly rebuts characterizations of her work as inconsistent or contradictory; his book persuasively identifies enduring and essential priorities around which her poetics coalesce. *Diane di Prima: Visionary Poetics and the Hidden Religions* also calls to account the tendency in literary scholarship to patronize hermetic topics or to nod briefly in their direction before lumping them into "mystical" or "visionary" categories that are left unexamined, their significance understated or ignored. To do so in di Prima's case, Calonne demonstrates, constitutes denial of who she is as a poet and activist. "Critics," di Prima asserts in a lecture he quotes in the book, avoid "the esoteric," wanting to "take part of the package and leave the rest, like let's take Newton's laws of mechanics and forget his alchemy." "The spiritual," she contends, "has got to come back" (195-96). Calonne's study does di Prima and her readers the service of revealing "the spiritual" in all its complexity as fundamentally constitutive of the full "package" of her life and work.

—Mary Paniccia Carden, Edinboro University of Pennsylvania

Works Cited

Butterick, George F. "Diane di Prima." *The Beats: Literary Bohemians in Postwar America. Dictionary of Literary Biography 16*, edited by Ann Charters, Gale, 1983, pp. 149-50.

Calonne, David Stephen. *The Spiritual Imagination of the Beats.* Cambridge UP, 2017.

di Prima, Diane. *Recollections of My Life as a Woman: The New York Years.* Viking, 2001.

Gair, Christopher. Review of *The Spiritual Imagination of the Beats*, by David Stephen Calonne. *Journal of Beat Studies*, vol. 7, 2019, pp.71-74.

Grace, Nancy M. and Ronna C. Johnson. "Pieces of a Song: Diane di Prima." *Breaking the Rule of Cool: Interviewing and Reading Beat Women Writers*, edited by Nancy M. Grace and Ronna C. Johnson, UP of Mississippi, 2004, pp. 83-106.

Knight, Brenda. "Diane di Prima: Poet Priestess." *Women of the Beat Generation: The Writers, Artists, and Muses at the Heart of a Revolution*, Conari, 1996, pp. 123-28.

Libby, Anthony. "Diane di Prima: 'Nothing Is Lost; It Shines in Our Eyes.'" *Girls Who Wore Black: Women Writing the Beat Generation*, edited by Ronna C. Johnson and Nancy M. Grace, Rutgers UP, 2002, pp. 45-68.

The Beat Index 2019

The Beat Index provides a chronicle of recent scholarship, including dissertations, in the field of Beat studies. The artists and other Beat generation figures represented here are core to the movement or are associated with then-contemporary and complementary avant-garde literary movements. Abstracts are included when available; these are publisher or author abstracts and may appear in excerpted form. Texts are organized alphabetically according to Beat or Beat-associated author. If we have omitted a title, such omission was unintentional, and we will greatly appreciate being informed of the omission so we can include it in the next volume of the *Journal*.

The Beat Generation

Belletto, Steven. *The Beats: A Literary History*. Cambridge UP, 2020.

> This critical history takes readers through key works by the major Beat authors, but also discusses dozens of other writers and their works, showing how they all contributed to one of the most significant literary movements of the post-World War II era. Moving from the early 1940s to the late 1960s, this book explores key aesthetic and thematic innovations of the Beat writers, the pervasiveness of the Beatnik caricature, the role of the counterculture in the postwar era, the involvement of women in the Beat project, and the changing face of Beat political engagement during the Vietnam War era.

Frey, Hugo. "Beat-Era Literature and the Graphic Novel." *The Cambridge History of the Graphic Novel*, edited by Jan Baetens, Hugo Frey, and Stephen E. Tabachnick. Cambridge UP, 2018.

Inchausti, Robert. *Hard to Be a Saint in the City: The Spiritual Vision of the Beats*. Shambala, 2018.

> Robert Inchausti explores the Beat canon to reveal that the movement at the heart of the Beat generation was a spiritual one. It goes deeper than the Buddhism with which many of the key figures became identified and is about their shared perception of an existence in which the Divine reveals itself in the ordinary. The book shows that theirs is a spirituality in which real life triumphs over airy ideals and personal authenticity becomes both the content and the vehicle for a kind of refurbished American Transcendentalism.

Lee, A. Robert. *The Beat: Authorships, Legacies*. Edinburgh UP, 2019.

> This book pairs close readings with a strong overview of the movement and ranges from women's Beat writing to African American Beats to the canonical texts, including "Howl," *On the Road*, and *Naked Lunch*. A closing chapter maps post-Beat writing and the ways Beat has morphed into new postmodern forms.

Mortenson, Erik. *Translating the Counterculture: The Reception of the Beats in Turkey*. Southern Illinois UP, 2018.

> In Turkey, the Beat message of dissent is given renewed life as publishers, editors, critics, readers, and others dissatisfied with the conservative social and political trends in the country have turned to the Beats and other countercultural forebears for alternatives. Through an examination of a broad range of literary translations, media portrayals, interviews, and other related materials, Mortenson seeks to uncover how the Beats and their texts are being circulated, discussed, and used in Turkey to rethink the possibilities they might hold for social critique today.

Amiri Baraka

Azouz, Samy. "Existence in Black and White: Theatrical Representation of the Varieties of Racism in Amiri Baraka's Select Plays." *Journal of African American Studies*, vol. 23, no. 3, 2019, pp. 147-61.

> In Baraka's drama, racism has two main forms: one is propositional and the other is dispositional. Propositional (extrinsic) racism conveys fierce racist behavior. Dispositional (intrinsic) racism is the expression of loyalty to the ethnic group and belonging to the community. The objective of this article is to address the construct of propositional racism and delineate its manifestations. It also tackles the concept of dispositional racism and highlights how it is connected to principles germane to morality and relevant to community.

Brown, Scot. "A Conversation with Amiri Baraka: Politics, Class Struggle and Black Culture (January 5, 1996)—A Retro-Engagement." *The Langston Hughes Review*, vol. 25, no. 2, 2019, pp. 179-95.

> In 1996, Scot Brown interviewed the prolific twentieth and twenty-first century writer, scholar and activist Amiri Baraka. Their dialogue focused on a crucial period in the history of the Black Arts and Black Power movements, between the later 1960s and early-1970s. During that period Baraka's organization, Committee For a Unified Newark (CFUN), participated in an alliance of Black cultural nationalist organizations that was heavily influenced by Maulana Karenga, chairman of the Us Organization. Brown's interview, then, focuses on a significant transitional period in Baraka's career when he, through praxis, became critical of cultural nationalism and moved toward a Marxist-Leninist-Maoist ideology of revolutionary change.

Casmier, Stephen. "Gassire's Heir: A Correspondence between Amiri Baraka (LeRoi Jones) and Robert Duncan." *MELUS*, vol. 44, no. 2, 2019, pp. 44-70.

> This essay explores the immemorial image of "Gassire's Lute" and the sacrificed poet's kingdom of Wagadu, which works as a background text to an exchange of three letters between Amiri Baraka and his friend Robert Duncan during the early 1960s, as they differently reinterpreted the pull of the ancient story and its structuring lessons about the roles of transcendent poet versus politically engaged writer-warrior. Following more than thirty years of neoliberal revision of the 1960s counterculture, the nuanced correspondence between the two friends about Baraka's 1963 poem "BLACK DADA NIHILISMUS" involves a densely packed discussion of aesthetics, cosmology, transcendence, transformation, community, theories of engagement, and even a sense of betrayal that presents a vibrant snapshot of a crucial moment in American history.

Crawford, Margo N. "The 'Atmos-Feeling' of Resurrection: Feeling Black (Not Slave) in Black Arts Movement Drama." *Modern Drama*, vol. 62, no. 4, 2019, pp. 483-501.

Krasner, David. "Expectation, Melancholy, and Loss: *Funnyhouse of a Negro* and *Dutchman* in the Year 1964." *Theatre Journal*, vol. 71, no. 1, 2019, pp. 49-67.

> Adrienne Kennedy's *Funnyhouse of a Negro* and Amiri Baraka's *Dutchman* were produced in 1964, during a period of paradigm

shifts in African American history. This essay examines the plays from the perspective of the historical background and social climate during the epicenter of the civil rights movement. Moreover, the essay argues that the protagonists of the plays were intellectuals beset by conflicting forces that impeded their desires for intellectual accomplishment and achievement.

Marcoux, Jean-Philippe, and Michael New. "Langston Hughes and Amiri Baraka: An Annotated Discography." *The Langston Hughes Review*, vol. 25, no. 2, 2019, pp. 196-223.

Schaag, Kathleen. "'Will Blackness Please Step Out and Take a Curtain Call?': Ed Bullins's Conceptual Theatre." *Modern Drama*, vol. 62, no. 3, 2019, pp. 272-91.

> Rereading Amiri Baraka's "The Revolutionary Theatre," Schaag reveals how the manifesto's Artaudian investment in a violent theatre of reality has distracted from Baraka's emphasis on the "vibrations of the mind in the world"; thus Schaag resists the tendency to privilege the embodied dimensions of black theatre more generally. Highlighting the quiet subtlety of Ed Bullins's and Baraka's texts, often overshadowed by the brashness and bravado associated with the Black Power movement, Schaag suggests that even the Black Theatre Movement's most dynamic revolutionary scripts encourage imaginative contemplation.

William S. Burroughs

Antonic, Thomas. "Genius and Genitality: William S. Burroughs Reading Wilhelm Reich." *Humanities*, vol. 8, no. 2, 2019, p. 101, doi.org/10.3390/h8020101. Accessed 21 May 2019.

> Antonic attempts to make visible all references to Wilhelm Reich in Burroughs's complete œuvre. The first section of the essay provides a brief biographical outline of Reich. In subsequent sections, Antonic describes how Burroughs and other Beat writers discovered Reich, how and to what extent Burroughs incorporated Reich in his texts, and what opinions Burroughs expressed about Reich in interviews and letters.

Johnston, Allan. "Teaching Magical Thinking: Notes Toward a Burroughsian Pedagogy." *Journal for the Philosophical Study of Education III*, 2018, pp. 184-201.

>Johnston addresses pedagogical practices that Burroughs used in writing classes, which exemplify some of the ideas that underlie his vision of the world, and particularly of the word, and stress how the forces of thought, perception, education, and existence shape our approach to daily life. These pedagogical approaches toward teaching writing perhaps parallel or supplement what Joseph Vecchio calls the "pedagogical ... sense" (vii) underlying much of Burroughs's experimentation with film and prose (the "cut-up" technique).

Miller, Gerald Alva, Jr. *Understanding William S. Burroughs* (Understanding Contemporary American Literature). U of South Carolina P, 2020.

>Through critical readings, Gerald Alva Miller, Jr. examines the life of William S. Burroughs and the evolution of his various radical styles in writing as well as audio, film, and painting. Miller argues that more than any other author Burroughs ushered in the era of both postmodern fiction and poststructural philosophy. Through this study, Miller situates Burroughs within the larger countercultural movements that began in the 1950s, when his novels became influential because of their examination of various control systems.

Weidner, Chad. "The Glorious Plagiarism, Trash Aesthetics, and Ecological Entropy of Cryptic Cut-Ups from Minutes to Go." *Humanities*, vol. 8, no. 2, 2019, p. 116, doi.org/10.3390/h8020116.

>This essay examines some of the ways in which select early cut-ups from *Minutes to Go* recall canonical literary forms, revive the revolutionary destructive urgency of Dada aesthetics, and contribute to wider environmental concerns. Weidner argues that unstudied examples of cryptic cut-ups from *Minutes to Go* participate in cultural recycling through the "Glorious Plagiarism" of canonical texts and that what emerges from the "Dada Compost Grinder" is a trash aesthetic highlighting the voids of both consumer and material culture.

Gregory Corso

Corso, Gregory. *Naropa Lectures 1981 (Part I & II)*. The CUNY Documents Initiative, 2016, www.centerforthehumanities.org/lost-and-found/publications/gregory-corso-naropa-lectures-1981.

Diane Di Prima

Braun, Jolie. "'Printing books shall eventually be my trade'": Piecing Together the History of Diane di Prima's Poets Press." *Tulsa Studies in Women's Literature*. Vol. 38, no. 2, 2019, pp. 425-33.

Davidson, Ian. "Times and Spaces Never Dreamed of in Diane di Prima's *Revolutionary Letters*." *Journal of Narrative Theory*, vol. 48, no. 3, 2018, pp. 314-338.

> Ian Davidson argues that rather than functioning as a form of individual consciousness-raising or heroic address, di Prima's Revolutionary Letters combines and sustains critical and discursive conversations between forms of poetry, revolutionary politics, and aesthetico-political philosophies that inform the work.

Kinniburgh, Mary Catherine. *The Shape of Knowledge: The Postwar American Poet's Library, with Diane di Prima and Charles Olson*. Dissertation. City University of New York, 2019.

> By exploring the Ralph Maud/Olson Library (a collection of every book Olson is believed to have read), Diane di Prima's occult library, and Diane di Prima's work as a publisher in her collection *Revolutionary Letters*, this dissertation establishes three main arguments. First, libraries that belong to poets are significant archival and conceptual units, which require specific institutional and scholarly approaches in order to be legible and indeed preserved. Second, that understanding these libraries as projects of how poets structure knowledge in postwar America offers us new insights into the question of the "postmodern," or information overload from an archival perspective. And third, that Diane di Prima warrants far more extensive critical study for her work at the intersection of multiple identities that make knowledge material: publisher, book collector, and indeed, alchemist.

Robert Duncan

Riou, Berengere. "Passages": *The Robert Duncan Centennial Conference in Paris.* Transatlantica, Sept. 2019.

> In June 2018, the Sorbonne hosted the Robert Duncan Centennial Conference to celebrate the birth of the poet and take stock of his ever-growing influence both in the field of English studies and in contemporary poetics. The idea for the conference came from the exchanges between the participants of the 2006 "(Re:)Working the Ground" Conference at Buffalo, New York.

McDowell, Tara. *The Householders: Robert Duncan and Jess.* The MIT Press, 2019.

> This study of the poet Robert Duncan (1919-88) and the artist Jess (1923-2004) examines the ways in which the couple negotiated issues of collaboration, nourishment, belonging, and power within the physical and conceptual household they shared, as well as a reading of the creative work they undertook from 1951 until 1980. The book toggles between close readings of Jess's artworks and Duncan's prose and poems and a narrative of their shared life, woven together with extensive archival research, interviews with more than a dozen of their intimates, and discussion of recent queer and feminist theory.

Lawrence Ferlinghetti

Collins, Ronald K. L. and David M. Skover. *The People v. Ferlinghetti: The Fight to Publish Allen Ginsberg's "Howl."* Rowan & Littlefield, 2019.

> The story of the obscenity trial surrounding Allen Ginsberg's "Howl" has often been told, but this study provides some additional information, including the unabridged 1957 judgment by Judge Clayton Horn (*People of the State of California v. Lawrence Ferlinghetti*, No. B27585) and a 2007 interview with Ferlinghetti, the publisher of Ginsberg's "Howl" and owner of the store raided by the police on June 3, 1957. This book includes a timeline, a list of printed and archival sources, copious notes, and a full index.

Woods, Gioia. *Left in the West: Literature, Culture, and Progressive Politics in the American West*. U of Nevada P, 2018.

> This book contains a chapter on Feringhetti: "'An International, Dissident, Insurgent Ferment': Lawrence Ferlinghetti and the Left Coast."

Allen Ginsberg

Ariel, Y. "From a Jewish Communist to a Jewish Buddhist: Allen Ginsberg as a Forerunner of a New American Jew." *Religions*, vol. 10, no. 2, 2019, p. 100.

> The article examines Allen Ginsberg's cultural and spiritual journeys, and traces the poet's paths as foreshadowing those of many American Jews of the last generation.

Ginsberg, Allen. *Conversations with Allen Ginsberg*, edited by David Calonne, U of Mississippi P, 2019.

> In this collection of interviews, Ginsberg discusses topics including censorship laws, the legalization of marijuana, and gay rights. The book also includes interviews that explore Ginsberg's interests in Buddhist philosophy, his intensive reading in a variety of spiritual traditions, the poet's relationship with Bob Dylan and the Beatles, and his various musical projects involving the adapting of poems by William Blake as well as settings of his own poetry.

Paris-Popa, Andreea. "The Madmen of Allen Ginsberg's 'Howl' and Their Blakean Roots." *British and American Studies*, vol. 25, 2019, pp. 161-71.

Shuchi, Israt J., and ABM Shafiqul Islam. "Reading Allen Ginsberg's 'September on Jessore Road': An Attempt to Ruminate Over the Horrific Reminiscences of the Liberation War of Bangladesh." *Advances in Language and Literary Studies*, vol. 10, no. 1, 2019, pp. 41-46.

> This essay addresses Allen Ginsberg's "September on Jessore Road," which captures the blood-stained history of the creation of Bangladesh through highlighting the unflinching struggle of the Bangladeshi people and their appalling plight during the country's war of independence in 1971. This poem mainly reports on

Ginsberg's visit to the refugee camps located in the bordering areas of Jessore, Bangladesh and Kolkata, India in mid-September 1971, while also criticizing the U.S. government and its state apparatus for not supporting the freedom-loving Bengalis in that war.

Tusler, Megan. "Caption, Snapshot, Archive: On Allen Ginsberg's Photo-Poems." *Criticism*, vol. 61, no. 2, Spring 2019, pp. 219-44.

Tusler attends primarily to images of William S. Burroughs and Gregory Corso in this essay. They appear as family and even as "one" in the photographs evaluated here, showing the fullest versions of community interrelations to which Ginsberg refers. The purpose of addressing these exemplars is to open up the possibilities for instability in intimacy as a way of forming affective community.

Jack Kerouac

De Saussure, Annie. "Satori in Brittany: Jack Kerouac, Youenn Gwernig, and the Breton Beat Novel." *Contemporary French and Francophone Studies*, vol. 22, no. 5, 2018, pp. 545-52.

Haynes, Sarah F. "Sad Paradise: Jack Kerouac's Nostalgic Buddhism." *Religions*, vol. 10, no. 4, 2019, p. 266, doi.org/10.3390/rel10040266.

Sarah Haynes considers the relationship between Kerouac's Buddhist practice and his multi-layered nostalgia. Based on a close reading of his unpublished diaries from the mid-1950s through mid-1960s, Haynes argues that Buddhism was a means of coping with his suffering and spiritual uncertainty. Kerouac's nostalgic Buddhism was a product of orientalist interpretations of the religion that allowed him to replace his idealized version of his past with an idealized form of Buddhism.

Käck, Elin "'Horrible Washing Sawing': Ecology and Anthropocentric Sublimity in Jack Kerouac's *Big Sur*." *Journal of Modern Literature*, vol. 43, no. 2, 2020, pp. 152-164.

The concept of the sublime informs Jack Kerouac's 1962 novel *Big Sur* in several ways, particularly the novel's engagement with ecocritical questions about consumption and the interrelationships between humans and nature. The novel paints a bleak portrait of nature, seemingly due to the inner turmoil of the main character, Jack Duluoz. Taking seriously the threatening aspects of *Big Sur* and reading them against the sublime and the Anthropocene reveal the novel's interrogation of the cost of human exploitation of the land, as well as its commitment to analyzing the complexities of the relationship between human and nonhuman, nature and artifact.

Keevil, Tyler. "Writing Kerouac's Bookmovie: Cinematic Influence and Imagery in the Modern Road Novel." *New Writing: The International Journal for the Practice and Theory of Creative Writing.* Vol. 14, no. 2, July 2017, pp. 167-175.

> This essay adopts a creative-critical approach in looking at the influence of cinema on the modern road novel. Through exploration of classic texts in the genre—Kerouac, Wolfe, and others—it demonstrates the extent of cinematic influence on the road novel's gestation and development. In particular, the essay examines Kerouac's concept of "the bookmovie" and seeks to establish just how prescient this has become. It posits that the author's own road novel, *The Drive*, fits the criteria of the "bookmovie" through its integration of cinematic homage, as well as its deployment of filmic style and technique.

McClure, John A. "Vitalist Nation: Whitman, Kerouac, Rand, DeLillo." *Christianity and Literature*, June 2018, vol. 67, no. 3, pp. 419-435.

Reesman, Jeanne C. "Fleeing the City: Authorial Self-Construction in Jack London's *The Road*, Jack Kerouac's *On the Road*, and Cormac McCarthy's *The Road*." *Studies in American Naturalism*, vol. 14, no. 1, 2019, pp. 104-25.

> This essay critiques *The Road* by Jack London, *The Road* by Cormac McCarthy, and *On the Road* by Jack Kerouac. Reesman discusses the inheritance of an ethos of personal survival matched with a sense of ethics and of community, the post-Darwinian awareness of the limitations of the human animal, and the writer's self-discovery in the book.

Winner, Kathryn. "*Visions of Cody* and Media: Jack Kerouac as Late Modernist." *Journal of Modern Literature*, vol. 43, no. 1, 2019, pp. 132-49.

> *Visions of Cody* is one of Jack Kerouac's most under-studied novels and his self-proclaimed masterpiece. Critics have often supposed that new technologies that feature so prominently in *Cody*'s experimentalism (tape recording, film, typewriting) are there to extend or augment Kerouac's devotion to central keywords in Kerouac studies: spontaneity, immediacy, physicality. Precisely to the contrary, *Cody*, the self-conscious descendant of Joycean literary modernism, is a record of anxiety about mediation, and an account of how literature fails—and perhaps must fail—to achieve "immediacy." This prompts the reconsideration of enduring constructions of Kerouac's authorship as sincerely devoted to instantaneous or spontaneous prose; it also prompts reexamination of the relevance of Beat writing to American receptions of modernism more broadly.

Joanne Kyger

Kyger, Joanne. *There You Are: Interviews, Journals, and Ephemera*, edited by Cedar Sigo. Wave, 2017.

> The inaugural book of Wave's new interview series, *There You Are* combines forty years of interviews, letters, poems, and journals to present a narrative of the poet Joanne Kyger, who intersected with the most influential movements of late twentieth-century poetry, yet remained rooted in her daily practice with a forthright attention to our present moment.

Charles Olson

Hand, Dominic. "Charles Olson's 'The Kingfishers' and Quantum Physics." *The Cambridge Quarterly*, vol. 48, no. 4, 2019, pp. 324-45.

> It was in "The Kingfishers" that Olson's immersion in the discourses of physics, and his treatment of quantum as a poetic substance, precipitated his radical formulations of a poetic methodology rooted in change and discovery. It is therefore essential to read "The Kingfishers" in light of the new epistemologies offered to Olson by

physics in support of his polemical aims to "go to the heart of your time, to shoot for the core." This essay seeks to elucidate some of the ways in which quantum physics, mathematics, and a context of new science affected Olson's processes of composition. Hand shows this through frequent comparisons between the final-form version of "The Kingfishers" and its working drafts, which he views as constellated worksheets for Olson's own ad-lib experiments with theories of universal space-time.

Shafer, Joseph R. "The Body of Space in Charles Olson's *Call Me Ishmael*." *The Arizona Quarterly*, vol. 75, no. 1, April 2019.

By introducing the body of space in *Call Me Ishmael*, through the book's re-narrativization of space, corresponding typographical or haptographical spacing, and concurrent poetry, this article discloses an aesthetics of fleshly space surfacing within and against the symbolic economy of *Call Me Ishmael*.

Kenneth Rexroth

Lihong, Zhu and Wang Feng. "The Zen Relationship between Chinese Poetry and American Poetry." *International Journal of Multicultural and Multireligious Understanding*, vol. 6, no. 4, 2019, pp. 92-101.

This article analyzes the poems of Kenneth Rexroth, Anthony Piccione, Gary Snyder, and James P. Lenfesty to explore the relationship between Chinese and American poetry. The authors argue that these poets imitate the quiet beauty, wild freedom, and orthodoxy of Zen poetry, thus creating a new realm of American poetry.

Gary Snyder

Byron, Mark. "Chinese Poetical Histories in Ezra Pound and Gary Snyder." *Critical Quarterly*, vol. 61, no. 1, 2019, pp. 99-114.

This essay considers specific poems by Pound and Snyder, arguably the two dominant figures in modern American poetry's attempt to reconcile itself to an idea of Chinese poetry and aesthetics. Both poets produced substantial translations of T'ang Dynasty poetry early in their careers: Pound with the publication of *Cathay* in 1915 and Snyder with his 24 "Cold Mountain Poems" in 1958. These texts and art objects also allow each poet to perform his own historical sensibility and demonstrate awareness of his place in American poetic history and its reception.

Lihong, Zhu and Wang Feng. "The Zen Relationship between Chinese Poetry and American Poetry." *International Journal of Multicultural and Multireligious Understanding*, vol. 6, no. 4, 2019, pp. 92-101.

> See abstract under Rexroth.

Philip Whalen

Ritvo, Mas. "'Since the Day I Was Kicked by Master Ma, I Have Not Stopped Laughing': Buddhism and Comedy in Philip Whalen." *Parnassus: Poetry in Review*, vol. 34, nos. 1-2, 2015, pp. 233-45.

> Buddhist comedy, which can be both strange-funny and laugh-out-loud funny, has a life beyond the records of medieval monks. The essay explores Buddhist comedy in the form of a koan and then investigates examples of such comedy in several of Whalen's poems.

In Memoriam

Michael McClure
(October 20, 1932 – May 4, 2020)

Photo credit: Brian Graham, 1988. Courtesy of the Allen Ginsberg Project.

The use of writing is not to lead out but to enact and create appendages of the body, of personal physiology. Making a radiance or darkness into an actual morphological part, an extension even. But more a physiological part. An action and an action to be known by.

Michael McClure, *Scratching the Beat Surface*

Essay Abstracts

"Take It Easier": Joanne Kyger in Bolinas
by Timothy Gray

This essay evaluates Joanne Kyger's move to Bolinas, California in the spring of 1969 as a key juncture in her literary development: as she pivots between movement and stasis, self and other, roaming and homecoming, open forms and grounded observations. While continuing to emphasize social freedoms celebrated by Beat writers, Kyger shifts much of her attention to the natural beauty of the California coast. Resolved to "take it easier," she fashions a creaturely story in which the self is part of other, non-human selves. The poet's relaxed pace and quirky humor, in keeping with her Buddhist practice, let her take it all in.

Joanne Kyger's Poetics: Finding the Continuous Thread
by Jane Falk

This essay investigates Joanne Kyger's poetic theories through a reading of her body of work, supplemented by her interviews as well as the influences of contemporaries and those she considers her lineage. Important aspects of such a poetics include lineation and the breath line, the serial poem, and open form. Techniques and practices Kyger gravitates to in the 1950s, 1960s, and 1970s inform her subsequent poetry, often demonstrating connections between her writing as a whole and Buddhist principles.

"Ted Talk"
by Aldon Lynn Nielsen

By the mid-1960s, the "hip" of the Beat era was edging into the "hippie," much to the confusion and consternation of America's culture watchers. This essay briefly explores the efforts of Marion Magid, a writer for *Esquire* magazine, who followed "hip" in search of its lingering traces. She took the same paths as hipster chronicler Ted Joans from the Village to Europe, but remained somewhat puzzled by what "hip" was in the process of becoming. Joans, though, equally persistent, gave us works such as *The Hipsters* and *All of Ted Joans and No More,* guidebooks to an alternative social order and surreal poetics.

Improvisation c. 1959: Beat Film
By Katherine Kinney

The faith in spontaneity characteristic of Beat literature was celebrated in four films understood as Beat in their moment: *Pull My Daisy* (Robert Frank and Albert Leslie 1959), *Shadows* (John Cassavetes 1959), *Guns of the Trees* (Jonas Mekas 1962), and *The Connection* (Shirley Clarke 1961). These films engendered a lively discussion regarding the nature, power, and failure of cinematic improvisation. Reconsidering these debates, Kinney argues that improvisation is not something that happens before the camera, but a variety of possibilities generated in relationship to the camera. Spontaneity is thus produced through forms of mechanical reproduction presumed to threaten it.

Notes on Contributors

Mary Paniccia Carden is professor of English and chairperson of the Department of English & Philosophy at Edinboro University of Pennsylvania, where she teaches courses in American literature. She is the author of *Women Writers of the Beat Era: Autobiography and Intertextuality* (U of Virginia P, 2018) and S*ons and Daughters of Self-Made Men: Improvising Gender, Place, Nation in American Literature* (Bucknell UP, 2010). Her essays on Diane di Prima, Joanne Kyger, and Jack Kerouac have appeared in *a/b: Auto/Biography Studies, Journal of Beat Studies,* and *Journeys*.

Jane Falk is retired from the University of Akron, where she served as a senior lecturer. Her research and scholarship focus on Joanne Kyger, Philip Whalen, Zen Buddhism and the Beats, and Beats and independent film.

Timothy Gray is professor of English at the College of Staten Island, City University of New York. In addition to *Moonchild*, a poetry chapbook (FootHills, 2013), he is the author of three critical studies, all published by University of Iowa Press: *Gary Snyder and the Pacific Rim: Creating Countercultural Community* (2006); *Urban Pastoral: Natural Currents in the New York School* (2010); and *"It's Just the Normal Noises": Marcus, Guralnick, No Depression, and the Mystery of Americana Music* (2017). His current book project, "Easy," offers an appraisal of 1970s pop music.

Allan Johnston teaches writing and literature at Columbia College Chicago and DePaul University. He co-edits *JPSE: Journal for the Philosophical Study of Education* and has published studies of the Beats and other writers in *Twentieth-Century Literature, College Literature, Review of Contemporary Fiction*, and other journals.

Katherine Kinney teaches twentieth-century American literature and film at the University of California Riverside. She is currently working on a book entitled *The Shock of Freedom: Movie Acting in the 1960s*. Her recent articles include "Facing the Camera: Black Actors and Direct Address in Independent Films of the 1960s" (*Journal of Cinema and Media Studies*, Fall 2019), "The Haunting of Don Draper" (*Pacific Coast Philology*, 2016), and "The Resonance of Brando's Voice" (*Postmodern Culture*, 2015).

Aldon Lynn Nielsen teaches at Central China Normal University and Penn State University. His collections of poetry include include *Heat Strings, Evacuation Routes, Stepping Razor, VEXT, Mixage, Mantic Semantic, A Brand New Beggar, Tray,* and *You Din't Hear This from Me*. He is the author of the critical studies *Black Chant and Integral Music*, among others.

John Shapcott is an honorary research fellow at Keele University. His writing on the Beats has appeared in the *Journal of American Studies* and *Beat Scene*. He has published numerous articles and book chapters on twentieth-century literature and silent movies, and has edited several critical volumes of the novels and stories of Arnold Bennett. He is the author of *Grains of Sand: Melvyn Bragg's Cumbria Novels* (Churnet Valley Books, 2015).

Tony Trigilio is the author of *Allen Ginsberg's Buddhist Poetics* (Southern Illinois UP, 2012) and editor of *Elise Cowen: Poems and Fragments* (Ahsahta Press, 2014). His most recent book of poetry is *Ghosts of the Upper Floor* (BlazeVOX Books, 2019). His selected poems, *Fuera del Taller del Cosmos*, was published in Guatemala in 2018 by Editorial Poe (translated by Bony Hernández). A founding member of the Beat Studies Association, he is a professor of English and Creative Writing at Columbia College Chicago.

Editorial Policy

The *Journal of Beat Studies* invites articles on the works of Beat movement writers and their colleagues, especially New York School, Black Mountain School, and San Francisco Renaissance writers, as well as those connected to these movements, in the United States and globally. The *Journal* intends to represent the breadth and eclecticism of critical approaches to Beat generation writers and welcomes new perspectives and contexts of inquiry.

The editors review all submissions, and if the submission is deemed to have publishing potential in the JBS, it is then sent for anonymous review to a member of the Editorial Board and at least one other external reader. Manuscripts should not be under consideration elsewhere, and we do not publish previously published work. It is strongly advised that those submitting work to *JBS* be familiar with the journal's content. Among criteria on which evaluation of submissions depends are whether an article demonstrates recognition of and thorough familiarity with scholarship already published in the field, whether the article is written clearly and effectively, and whether it makes a genuine contribution to Beat studies.

Preparation of Copy

1. Articles are typically between 25 and 30 pages, and do not exceed 9000 words, including notes and works cited. Inquiries about significantly shorter or longer submissions should be sent to the editors.

2. A separate page should include the article's title, author's name, address, telephone & fax numbers, e-mail address, and a 100-word professional biography. The author's name and identifying references should not appear on the manuscript to preserve anonymity for our readers.

3. All submissions must include an abstract of no more than 250 words.

4. The manuscript should be in Times New Roman 12, double-spaced, and should adhere to the most recent MLA style.

5. Submissions may be sent by email as Word documents to Ronna C. Johnson (ronna.johnson@tufts.edu) and Nancy M. Grace (ngrace@wooster.edu) simultaneously.

6. Submissions may also be sent via the online submission form at http://www.beatstudies.org/jbs/submission_guidelines.html.

7. Authors of accepted manuscripts are responsible for any necessary permissions fees and for securing any necessary permissions.

8. All editorial and review inquiries should be addressed to ronna.johnson@tufts.edu and ngrace@wooster.edu simultaneously.

9. Inquiries concerning orders and advertising exchanges should be addressed to PaceUP@pace.edu.

The eighth volume of the *Journal of Beat Studies*
was published in Spring 2020
by Pace University Press

Cover and Interior Layouts by Delaney Anderson and Francesca Leparik
The journal was typeset in Times New Roman and AmerType Md BT
and printed by Lightning Source in La Vergne, Tennessee

Pace University Press

Director: Manuela Soares
Associate Director: Stephanie Hsu

Graduate Assistants: Delaney Anderson and Francesca Leparik
Graduate Student Aide: Shani Starinsky

www.ingramcontent.com/pod-product-compliance
Lightning Source LLC
Chambersburg PA
CBHW061416300426
44114CB00015B/1956